BEYOND
ATKINS

What People Are Saying About Dr. Doug's *Total Health*...

I first met Dr. Doug at a speech he gave to the Rotary Club of Cincinnati. I've dedicated my whole life to saving lives and applaud his efforts in helping people take control of their health. The information set forth through his Total Health program can literally help save people's lives!

-Dr. Henry Heimlich physician/humanitarian,
*Developer of the Heimlich Maneuver
and Founder of the Heimlich Institute*

Dr. Doug's Total Health program has helped to enlighten our employees on health issues related to obesity. I'm a personal believer in his well-balanced approach to a protein-rich, favorable-carbohydrate way of eating. His program also helped me take off the few extra pounds I gained after my second child!

-Dr. Marleece Barber, physician,
Medical Director of Lockheed Martin Space Systems/NASA

"One of the biggest fiscal challenges of any self-insured company are the health costs associated with obesity. Over 50% of our yearly medication costs are related to high blood pressure, high cholesterol, and adult-onset diabetes. We're presently in the process of implementing Dr. Doug's *Total Health* program to help get the weight off of our employees to improve their health, productivity and our company's financial health through the reduction of medications associated with obesity-related conditions."

-Troy Leinen director of human resources, *Bombardier/Lear Jet*

"When I met Dr. Doug over 5 years ago, I was 20 pounds over weight and my cholesterol was close to 300. The head of cardiology was very concerned due to my high stress levels associated with managing a major hospital. I followed Dr. Doug's Total Health principles and lost the 20 pounds in less than 3 months and my cholesterol lowered by over 100 points without medication!"

-**Robert Shaw** chief executive officer, *Los Robles Regional Medical Center, Columbia/HCA*

"As a Registered Nurse specializing in occupational health issues, I'm always looking for a balanced approach on educating our employees to take better control of their health. Dr. Doug's Total Health approach to achieve optimum health and wellness by a combining a protein-rich, favorable-carbohydrate way of eating with regular exercise, intellectual development, and spiritual growth was just what the doctor ordered!"

-**Rosalind McNally, R.N.**, SCM, OHNC occupational health nurse, *Medical Services, Rockwell Scientific*

"As a registered dietician, I've always been skeptical of the Atkin's type of high protein diets. I'm a believer in protein-rich diets, but there needs to be a healthy balance of fats, portion-control, and carbohydrates in the form of fiber-rich vegetables, as well as fruits during weight loss. Dr. Doug's Total Health protein-rich, favorable-carbohydrate way of eating is the perfect balanced approach that I recommend for many of my patients."

-**Cynthia D. Langford,** R.D. registered dietician, *Renal Dialysis Centers*

"As a doctor specializing in family practice, I'm always looking for simple and effective ways to help my patients live healthier lives. That's why I always recommend the well-balanced, simple approach of Dr. Doug's Total Health program."

-**Dr. Francis M. Dawson** physician/family practice, *Board Certified Graduate of the UCLA School of Medicine*

"Dr. Doug gave a very informative and dynamic presentation to our employees during a visit to our corporate headquarters last year. His Total Health principles have helped many of our employees gain control of their health. As the chairman of the wellness committee, I'm always looking for a healthy, balanced and simple approach to educating our employees about wellness. As a concerned mother, I'm now implementing Dr. Doug's Total Health principles with my teenage athlete son."

-Barbara Essie, wellness chairman,
American Family Insurance Group

"My wife and I are following many of Dr. Doug's Total Health principles in our own lives. As the executive director of a health insurance company, I'm always looking for ways to keep our insured healthier. The reduction of monthly medication costs, expensive medical procedures, etc. helps our insurance company remain financially sound! I'm looking forward to implementing Dr. Doug's Total Health principles with our insured. "

-Richard Hare, executive director,
Tri-County Schools Insurance Group

"Dr. Doug was a guest author last March. After listening to his presentation I was convinced that carbohydrates were killing me! I went on his Total Health program online at www.totalhealthdoc.com and lost 30 pounds so quickly and easily in just 4 months. I now weigh 95 pounds and have kept it off since July. I work out three times a week and have gone from 25% body fat to 20% and I'm going to be 53 Years old in March! What is even more important is how much better I feel and all the energy I have now!"

-Sherry Klinkner, community relations manager,
Barnes & Noble Booksellers

BEYOND
ATKINS*

A Healthier, More Balanced Approach to a Low Carbohydrate Way of Eating

DR. DOUGLAS J. MARKHAM

Foreword by Larry King

Total Health Care Publishing
Westlake Village, California

Care has been taken to ensure the accuracy of the information presented herein and to describe generally accepted practices. However, the author, editor, and publisher are not responsible for errors or omissions or for any consequences from the application of the information in this book and make no warranty, express or implied, with regard to the contents of the book.

Further, as new scientific information becomes available through basic and clinical research and studies, recommended treatments and procedures undergo changes. Thus, although the author, editor, and publisher have done everything reasonably possible to make this book accurate and up-to-date, current procedures, methods and practices are dynamic and subject to change. In addition, individual anatomy, physiology, requirements and capabilities vary and specific recommendations applicable in general may not be appropriate for a particular individual. Lastly, this book is not intended to be taken as medical advice nor to supplant appropriate medical consultation, but rather it is intended to be educational. In view of all of the foregoing, the reader is therefore advised to always consult with his or her physician or other appropriate health and fitness professional regarding these matters.

First Edition

Library of Congress Control Number: 2003095466
ISBN: 0-9701710-8-0

Markham, Douglas J.
    Beyond Atkins: A Healthier More Balanced Approach to a Low
    Carbohydrate Way of Eating /
    by Douglas J. Markham.
        -- 1st ed.
        p. cm.
    Includes bibliographical references and index.
        ISBN: 0-9701710-8-0
        1. Health. 2. Nutrition. 3. Physical fitness. I. Title.
        RA76.M37 2004 613.7

Dedication

To my wife and best friend, Andrea R. Gasporra, D.D.S. for her never-ending love, patience and continued understanding.

To my mother, Loretta Markham, a single-parent who gave the best years of her young-life to raise her four children on minimum wages.

For my grandmother, Mary Markham, who was born on a Wisconsin farm in 1898 and who lived to age 94. Her stories, guidance, and family values continue to influence and inspire me.

To Bruce and Helen Timm, the neighbors whose love and generosity made all the difference in a young boy's life.

To the over 300,000 victims and their families, loved-ones, friends, co-workers, etc., who die of obesity-related diseases every year.

To my patients, for without their support, belief, compliance and commitment to my Total Health program, there would be no book.

To my loyal staff, Beverly Donley and Gretchen Linville, whose unwavering support for me and our patients, will never be forgotten.

Table of Contents

Acknowledgements

I want to express my gratitude to the many people who made this book possible, starting with my patients, staff and friends, who urged me to share the *Total Health* weight loss and wellness program with the rest of the world.

This book would not exist without their unwavering support. In particular, I'd like to thank the people whose time, talent and dedication helped shape and polish the pages that follow.

My deepest gratitude goes to Larry King, author, show host, and founder of the Larry King Cardiac Foundation, who despite the enormous demands made upon him, found the time to contribute an eloquent and thoughtful foreword expressing the importance of taking control of your health. He has always been a special source of inspiration and encouragement to all of us through his fair and balanced approach to covering our world's events.

Henry Heimlich, M.D., developer of the Heimlich maneuver, founder of the Heimlich Institute, humanitarian and fellow Rotarian, for the review of this manuscript and much more importantly his contributions to the human race. His life's contributions have probably saved more lives than any individual in the history of humankind through his innovative life-saving techniques.

Thanks to U.S. Secretary of Health, Tommy Thompson, and our Surgeon General, Richard Carmona, M.D., for their administration's commitment to fighting obesity. Also to Tommy Thompson's and my fine home state of Wisconsin, for providing us with a wholesome environment and an excellent public education system during our childhood years.

A special thanks to my good friend John Schneider, actor/director, whose inspirational story of overcoming childhood obesity has inspired millions of people. Also for his enthusiasm and support to me and my efforts to enlighten society about the pitfalls of obesity-related diseases.

Frank M. Dawson, M.D., family practice, for his continued friendship and his tireless commitment to his patients and community service work with the Conejo Free Clinic.

A big thank you to my friend Jackson Sousa, exercise physiologist and personal trainer, for his review of the exercise section of this book and getting me into shape as my personal trainer.

Thank you to Cynthia Langford, registered dietician, for her support and review of the nutritional concepts that make the *Total Health* protein-rich, favorable- carbohydrate way of eating a well-balanced success.

Thanks to Stephen G. Axelrode, D.O., family practice, Chief of Primary Care, Los Robles Regional Medical Center, Miguel Gonzalez, M.D., internal medicine, and Mel Hyashi, M.D., orthopedist, for their patient referrals and professional feedback.

I am also grateful to Troy Leinen, manager of human resources and Karen Lehman, R.N., occupational health services of Bombardier Aerospace/Lear Jet, for supporting *Total Health* as an employee benefit and internet-based corporate wellness program.

Thanks to Robert Shaw, chief executive officer, Los Robles Regional Medical Center, for helping me introduce the *Total Health* program to the medical community and to his wife, Lisa, who has championed *Total Health*'s benefits to youth through local Parent Teacher's Associations.

Special thanks to my friend Marc Colen, intellectual property attorney, for his direction, guidance, and friendship throughout my various projects.

Thanks to Tom Voccola and Francis Fuji, co-founders of CEO2, for their support, friendship and corporate visioning principles which have helped to shape and polish my life's purpose, goals, and dreams.

Multitudes of gratitude must be given to Tracy Ging, director of marketing and Leanna Mix, public relations, of *DaVinci Gourmet* and Roeland Polet, vice-president of marketing, *Carbolite Foods*, for their belief in the *Total Health* program and their company's monetary support, moral support and continued commitment to the *HEALTH* Across America campaign. Also for both of their company's dedication to producing the finest sugar-free and low carbohydrate products available.

A heart-felt thanks goes to Matt Russell of *Russell Public Affairs Group*, for his friendship, public relations talents, editorial direction and boundless enthusiasm for this program and its ability to change people's lives.

Foreword

Dr. Doug Markham is an incredible young man. I first met him when he was a guest on my television show and found his thoughts and presentation most impressive.

I then received an advance copy of this book, "Beyond Atkins: A Healthier More Balanced Approach to a Low Carbohydrate Way of Eating". It is certainly among the best printed material ever about the subject of good health, diabetes control and balanced living.

I've lost weight, my blood sugar levels are generally below 100, which is remarkable for someone with type 2 diabetes, which I have. I have reduced the amount of supportive prescription medications I've been taking and I'm on my way to eliminating them completely.

His exercise program makes a lot of sense and isn't difficult.

If you follow what Dr. Doug advises, I can almost guarantee you will lead a better, healthier life.

Go get'em!

Larry King

Introduction

The idea behind the *Total Health* program is that you have the absolute right to health and happiness. You work hard to provide for yourself and your loved ones. Compromise and sacrifice are part of life. Unfortunately, it's all too easy to compromise your physical and mental health along the way.

And that's a crime. Because if you've sacrificed your health, you'll end up spending your hard-earned resources on medical bills treating a lifetime of poor health choices. It's hard to enjoy the fruits of your labor when the lifestyle you've worked so hard for is limited by deteriorated health.

The *Total Health* program has inspired and enlightened individuals to achieve optimum health and wellness by combining a protein-rich, favorable-carbohydrate way of eating with regular physical exercise, intellectual development, and spiritual growth.

Thousands of people have participated in the *Total Health* program, with many of them no longer needing prescription medications for diseases such as high blood pressure, high cholesterol, and adult-onset diabetes.

It's my sincere belief that everyone has the absolute right to be both healthy and happy. People just need the right tools to help empower them to effect change.

In July 2002, John Schneider and I appeared together on *CNN's* "*Larry King Live*" where John came out for the first time on national television to share his struggle with childhood obesity. I also announced my plans to depart on my "*HEALTH Across America Tour,*" part of a national public education campaign on the prevention of obesity-related diseases. This tour will eventually take me to America's 25 "fattest cities" as ranked by *Men's Fitness* magazine.

At age 16, with a 44-inch waist and weighing just under 250 pounds, John heeded the advice of his brother and began making lifestyle changes. Two years and 50 pounds later, John's acting career took him to the top, being cast as the heart throb Bo Duke on television's *"Dukes of Hazard."* John currently stars on the *WB hit television series "Smallville,"* and subscribes to the *Total Health* weight Loss and wellness management philosophy.

The idea for an expanded version of my first book *Total Health*, resulted from the overwhelming response to John's inspirational story and my continued commitment to fighting childhood and adult obesity. The goal of this book is to enlighten the world with a simple, safe, and effective answer to gaining control of your weight loss, wellness and fitness goals.

Remember, it's your absolute right to be healthy and happy! It's my sincere and deepest desire that this book and the Total Health *program helps you take your first steps towards taking control of your health and a lifetime of health and happiness!*

Yours in *Total Health*,

Dr. Doug

P.S. - Even though the *Total Health* program is a much more balanced approach to a *low carbohydrate way of eating*, I must give thanks to the pioneers of protein-based diets.

Pioneers like Dr. Stillman, Dr. Atkins and others who despite the ridicule of their peers and the nutritional establishment remained true to their beliefs.

They were always on the right track, but their approaches were not well-balanced enough.

What You Will Discover

1. **Part I: Five Key Talking Points for Taking Control of Your Health:** This chapter will explain *Why the Classic Low-fat Diet has been a Miserable Failure, Why Fat does Not Make You Fat and How Obesity has Become the Leading Cause of Preventable Death.* We will also look at *How the Food Industry is Largely Responsible for the Obesity Epidemic* and *Why the Food Pyramid Should be Turned Upside Down.*

We will explore *How Food Acts Like a Drug,* and how the kind of food you eat has a tremendous affect on your body, your energy level, your mental alertness and the quality of your life. The bottom line: The kind of food you eat and the amount of food you eat and when you eat it tells your body whether to burn fat or store fat.

We will also explain *How to use Food to Help your Medical Doctor Potentially Reduce or Eliminate Medications for High Blood Pressure, High Cholesterol and Adult-Onset Diabetes.* You will discover *Why the Total Health program is More Effective than the Zone Diet and More Well-Balanced than the Atkins Diet.*

2. **Part II: Eating Your Way to Health:** You will discover *the safest and most effective way to follow a low-carbohydrate lifestyle.* This includes the right balance of carbohydrates, protein and fat based on the *Total Health* program to boost energy, lose weight and stay healthy.

This section also includes *prepared meal menu options* based on the reader's body frame size and fat burning goals according to the

Total Health protein-rich, favorable-carbohydrate way of eating. *Macronutrient food unit lists of the most favorable protein and carbohydrate choices* are provided in this section. We'll inform you on *How to Choose the Right Vitamin and Mineral Supplement* along with *insightful Facts on Fiber, Water, Digestive Disorders and "Silo Syndrome."*

3. Part III: Exercise: How to Get Started and Why. You will also discover *how a combination of aerobic, resistance and passive exercise will make your body stronger and keep it working longer. I'll give you insider tips on choosing a health club and working with a personal trainer.*

I will also share the training techniques that I developed during my high school All-American wrestling days, which were based on circuit training exercise. Arthur Jones, the inventor of Nautilus fitness equipment, first introduced circuit-training concepts back in the 1970's, which are now becoming popular once again.

I will explain the *principles behind circuit training* along with a section of photographs of performing proper warm-up and stretching exercises. This section will also include photographs and instructions on performing my *30 Minute " Fat Burning" Circuit Training Workout*™. I developed this unique exercise system to be performed at home or on the road using a bungee resistance exercise band.

30 Minute " Fat Burning" Circuit Training Workout™ consists of working out all the major muscle groups by performing 9 different exercises. These include the back, stomach, shoulders, arms, legs, and chest. You perform 3 sets of 12 repetitions of each exercise in addition to walking or running in place with the resistance of the bungee device for 30 seconds in between each set of exercises.

4. Part IV: Mental Health: Helpful Hints for Happiness. One of the keys to *Total Health* is that *your mental health is just as important as your physical health.* This chapter offers a few thoughts about the importance of exercising that big muscle between your ears! I constantly try to instill the thought that *you have the absolute right to be healthy and HAPPY.* I will share some tips on *how to* *preserve your emotional and social well-being and the importance of intellectual and spiritual growth.*

5. **Part V: Total Health Success Stories:** Need some inspiration or motivation? The *Total Health* program is working for everyday people every day! In this section, you'll read the stories of six patients who changed their lives using the *Total Health* program.

6. **Part VI: Total Health Recipes:** This section will give you some tasty *meat, pork and poultry, fish and seafood, vegetable and protein-rich snack recipes* based on the *Total Health* protein-rich, favorable-carbohydrate way of eating.

7. **Appendix I: Contract for Health and Happiness.** Here's one contract you won't have to run by your attorney. This will be your personal contract for health and happiness. You'll be encouraged to make a copy of this contract, sign it, and read it daily. It will be used to reaffirm your desire and commitment to live in *Total Health* and renew your pledge to participate in life to the best of your abilities.

8. **Appendix II: Total Health Before & After Photos:** In this section, you'll see dramatic before & after pictures of real-life *Total Health* participants.

9. **Appendix III: John Schneider Before & After Photos/Larry King Appearance:** This section includes some of John's childhood obesity pictures along with our appearance on the set of *CNN's "Larry King Live."*

10. **Appendix IV: HEALTH Across America Tour Photos:** This section shows a few highlights from my *"HEALTH Across America Tour,"* part of a national public education campaign on the prevention of obesity-related diseases. This tour will eventually take me to America's 25 "fattest cities" as ranked by *Men's Fitness* magazine.

Part I

Five Key Talking Points for Taking Control of Your Health

1. The fact about the classic low-fat, high-carbohydrate diet that we have been recommended to follow over the past 20 years is that <u>it simply does not work</u>!

The American public is 32% fatter than we were 20 years ago. About 1 out of 3 adults and now 1 out of 8 children is considered clinically obese. Obesity contributes to an estimated 300,000 deaths every year and is surpassing smoking as the leading cause of preventable of death. More than $100 billion is spent on obesity-related expenses in the United States each year, not including the $42.6 billion spent annually to shed excess weight. Over 53.6 million workdays are lost every year to obesity-related diseases and American businesses are losing more than $4 billion per year in lost productivity.

Now if you go by results, like I do, those are not very good results. The reason that the low-fat, high-carbohydrate diet does not work is simple, FAT DOES NOT MAKE YOU FAT! That's right! Contrary to what nutritionists and the food industry have been spouting for decades, eating fat is not the reason so many Americans are overweight. The real culprit is the high carbohydrate content of our diets. I grew up in the state of Wisconsin and we did not fatten the pigs and cows with fat, we fattened them with low-fat grain. The same foods the nutritional establishment has been telling us to eat over the past 20 years!

The way to fully understand why fat does not make you fat and low-fat grains do, is to take a look at the dietary hormonal connection and how food acts as a drug.

2. Food Is A Drug: The Hormonal Connection. The kind of food you eat has a tremendous affect on your body, your energy levels, your mental alertness and the quality of your life. Like a drug, the food you eat causes powerful biochemical reactions in your body. The bottom line: The kind of food you eat and when you eat it tells your body whether to burn fat or store fat.

How is food like a drug? First, like a drug, food can be very addictive. Second, like a drug, food causes strong biochemical reactions in your body. And finally, like a drug, food can be used or abused. We all know how easy it is to abuse food.

For many people, there are strong psychological forces behind their eating behavior. Those issues need to be worked out with professional help. But, the impulse to eat certain kinds of foods is not all in your head. When you get the craving for those M&Ms in the bottom right hand drawer, there's some serious biochemistry at work, too.

The Hormonal Connection

Hormones are chemicals manufactured by special glands in your body and released into your bloodstream. Your blood transports hormones to different parts of your body, where hormones influence the way organs and tissues work. Because hormones control and influence so many vital processes, such as, growth, sexual drive, aging and your metabolism to name a few, hormone research is one of the most exciting fields of medical science.

Among the scientific research to emerge from these studies is the strong connection between food and hormones. Specifically, the kind of food you eat and how much you eat triggers the release of two powerful hormones, insulin and glucagon.

What you may ask is so important about insulin and glucagon? The answer is simple: *Insulin tells your body to store fat. Glucagon tells your body to burn fat.* Therefore we want to produce more fat burning *glucagon* and less fat storing *insulin.*

The Dangers of Excess Insulin

When you eat foods that produce too much insulin, not only are you telling your body to store fat, all that excess insulin boosts production of triglycerides or blood fats. And what does blood fat do to your arteries? It clogs them, which makes you a prime candidate for a stroke or heart attack.

Excess insulin also stimulates the liver to produce cholesterol. This is why your cholesterol levels can still be high even if you cut all the fats out of your diet. The amount of fat you eat does not influence your blood cholesterol levels that much. The real culprit is excess insulin, which also contributes to high blood pressure.

I've saved the worst for last. When your body produces excess insulin on a regular basis, you are likely to develop insulin resistance. This is a vicious cycle where the body becomes less sensitive to insulin and compensates by secreting more and more of the stuff.

The result: You store more and more fat and gain more and more weight. After awhile, your pancreas, which produces insulin, cannot satisfy the demand. This is a precursor to acquiring a deadly disease called adult onset diabetes.

Adult onset diabetes, also known as type II diabetes, affects more than eight million Americans. It is a devastating disease characterized by loss of energy and weight gain. People afflicted with diabetes suffer blindness, heart disease, kidney failure and circulatory problems that often lead to the amputation of fingers and toes. Diabetes is also a well-known cause of male impotency.

Scared? You should be. It's estimated that there are another eight million Americans who suffer from some form of diabetes and don't even know it!

The Good News

Now, take a deep breath. There is a proven way to get your body to reduce the amount of fat-storing insulin and promote the release of fat-burning glucagon. And you don't need expensive prescription medicines or pre-packaged meals. The secret is to eat the right combination of everyday foods, in the right amount, at the right time.

Understanding the Right Combination of Food

Whether your goal is to decrease body fat, and increase energy, or get sick less often, the key to success starts with the proper combination of food. The body has the complex task of managing a host of intricate functions to promote life and harmony. To do this the body needs fuel.

The body extracts fuel through a highly complex network of chemical reactions which begin with the digestion of food. Smaller compounds formed from the breakdown of food are then metabolized into the simple compounds, water, carbon dioxide, and oxygen which is easily disposed of by the body. During this process of metabolism body fuel is formed.

All food is composed of macronutrients (protein, carbohydrates, and fat), micronutrients (vitamins and minerals), and water. Apart from water, food is primarily made up of macronutrients. Macronutrients are the only food components that provide food energy, measured as calories, to maintain life.

Carbohydrates are different forms of simple sugars linked together in polymers (chains). Carbohydrates are found in the form of bread, pasta, rice, potatoes, fruits, juices, vegetables and sweets. When you eat carbohydrate-rich foods, your body converts them into glucose, also known as blood sugar. Very little carbohydrate is actually required other than the amount needed for additional calories to provide energy to the body and to nourish the tissues that require it - red blood cells, parts of the eye, the kidneys and the brain.

Protein comes in the form of beef, pork and poultry, fish and seafood, soy protein, and dairy products such as eggs and cheese. Protein is made of amino acids, the building blocks that your body uses to make up your lean body mass (muscles), hair, skin, nails and eyes. Nine of these amino acids, known as the essential amino acids, can not be synthesized by your body and must be supplied by a high-quality protein.

Fat is found in high amounts in dairy products such as butter, cheese and eggs. We also see it on the edge of red meat and it's found in nuts and oils. The important thing to know about fat is that *fat does not make you fat!* In fact, you need the *right kind* of fat in your diet in the *right* amount to burn fat and produce hormones essential to good health.

The Hormonal Response to Food

The reason excess carbohydrate consumption leads to obesity has to do with your body's hormonal response to food. Here's what happens when you eat a meal that is loaded with carbohydrates.

When you eat a high-carbohydrate meal, like pasta or French toast or a half a box of Ding Dongs, those carbs are rapidly converted into glucose or blood sugar. As a result, your blood sugar levels surge. At first, this makes your brain very happy. The brain is a glucose hog and consumes about two-thirds of the glucose in your body for energy.

The spike in blood sugar also triggers your pancreas to secrete insulin. Remember, insulin's job is to reduce the amount of glucose in the bloodstream. It does this by storing excess glucose. First, a small amount is stored in your liver and muscles. The rest of the excess glucose is stored as body fat.

But it's not over yet. As I said, the brain craves glucose. And when insulin does its job to reduce excess glucose, there isn't enough glucose left for the brain to convert into energy. This is why you start to nod off after a big carb-heavy meal.

So, the brain sends a message: consume more carbohydrates! That's when you reach for your mid-morning or mid-afternoon stash of M&Ms. That's how you end up taking a ride on the blood sugar roller coaster, cycling dramatically from high to low energy. And that's how all those excess carbs become excess pounds. It's a vicious cycle that leads to obesity, insulin resistance, hypoglycemia and worse.

> *The secret to breaking this cycle and taking control of your health is simple: Increase the amount of protein you eat and decrease the amount of carbohydrates.*

Eating the right amount of protein stimulates the release of glucagon, a hormone that helps stabilize your energy levels by mobilizing the release of the sugars stored in your liver to satisfy your brain's need for glucose. (Thus, curbing and eventually ending your carbohydrate cravings.) Another bonus: Glucagon also helps your body burn stored body fat!

So instead of eating French toast for breakfast, have an omelet with fresh fruit. Instead of pasta for lunch, eat chicken, beef, fish or your favoraite protein entrée with vegetables. So normally when you would be reaching for your mid-morning or mid-afternoon stash of M&Ms to satisfy you brain's cravings for sugar to increase your energy levels, you're burning stored fat and the stored sugars in your liver for energy rather than taking a ride on the "blood sugar roller-coaster!"

So this is how food acts like a drug! There's not a drug company in the whole world, with unlimited financial resources and the top scientists, who could create a drug that could do a better job regulating your blood sugars, burning stored body fat and increasing your energy levels than the kind of food you eat, how much you eat, and when you eat it!

Now don't get me wrong. I'm not saying all carbohydrates are bad for you. Carbohydrates are an essential part of healthy nutrition, as long as you eat the right amount and the right kind.

What makes one form of carbohydrate better than another? The answer is a carbohydrate's *glycemic index* - the rate at which a carbohydrate is converted into glucose, or sugar, in the bloodstream. *High-glycemic carbs* convert into sugar rapidly, causing an increased insulin response. *Low-glycemic carbs* convert into sugar at a slower rate, resulting in a reduced insulin response.

"Good" carbohydrates are *low-glycemic* carbohydrates. "Bad" carbohydrates are *high-glycemic* carbohydrates. If you want to live in *Total Health*, it is essential that you choose to eat good carbohydrates over bad carbohydrates whenever possible.

Virtually all fiber-rich fruits and vegetables are *low-glycemic* except for carrots, corn, dried fruits, and bananas. You also want to limit other carbohydrates that convert rapidly into sugar, such as bread, pasta, rice, and potatoes. These foods are not entirely forbidden, but the less of them you eat, the better you'll feel.

Note: See the complete *Macronutrient Food Unit* list of *low-glycemic* carbohydrates in the chapter **Eating Your Way To Health.**

The Truth About Burning Fat (Ketosis)

There is a difference between starvation, prolonged fasting and controlled carbohydrate eating. There are similar metabolic mechanisms at work, but the differences are key to understanding the safety and efficacy of controlled carbohydrate diets.

The whole process of muscle protein catabolism and liver gluconeogenesis is regulated principally by glucocorticosteroids and glucagon and a relative lack of insulin. Early in fasting glycogen reserves are depleted, and protein (mainly from muscle) becomes the major source of carbon for glucose production. Glucose is required in substantial amounts by blood cells and the central nervous system on a daily basis. There is also an initiation of ketone body production by the liver to provide a more water soluble form of fat-derived fuel.

A very similar adaption of protein and energy metabolism occurs in persons consuming diets very low in carbohydrates, where there is little or no glycogen reserve. However, in this instance, *dietary protein* largely or fully substitutes for muscle protein in gluconeogenesis.

Note: "Dietary protein largely or fully substitutes for muscle protein in gluconeogenesis."

Even when discussing starvation most critics of low carb diets miss the boat. The body adapts to starvation and reduces the need for protein-dependent gluconeogenesis by boosting its production of ketones, a fuel alternative to glucose for most cells.

Circulating ketones reach maximum levels after about ten days of fasting and now substitute for much of the glucose requirement of the central nervous system. This drastically reduces the need for catabolism of muscle protein.

With reduced protein catabolism, urinary nitrogen excretion also declines. And there is a shift from the excretion of urea to a predominance of ammonia loss. This shift toward ammonia versus urea parallels the increased production and excretion of keto acids, and serves to maintain acid/base balance.

The overall point is that muscle is a valuable reserve of carbons that can be used for glucose production when needed. However the body prevents excessive losses of muscle protein over long periods of fasting by adapting the central nervous system to utilization of ketone bodies for fuel."

The good news for low-carb followers:

A parallel adaptation in the production and excretion of ammonium ions by the kidney neutralizes the increased ketone bodies (principally beta-hydroxybutyric and acetoacetic acids). Without the latter adaptation, such large productions of keto acids would cause a severe ketoacidosis, as well as a loss of large quantities of sodium and potassium ions (accompanying ketones spilled into the urine).

Therefore, unless one is an insulin dependent diabetic or literally starving to death due to a lack of food, there is little or no danger from ketosis which is not characterized by a simultaneous rise in blood glucose and blood acidity.

Why Fat is the Key to Good Health

Contrary to the nutritional "wisdom" most of us get from the media and food packaging, not all fat is bad for you. In fact, your body needs a certain amount of fat to nourish cells, supply essential fatty acids, and to trigger the release of a hormone that signals your brain that you're full. Fat also slows down the conversion of carbohydrates into glucose, feeding your brain a study flow of glucose, not a sudden rush that triggers an excess insulin response.

Most importantly, eating the *right kind* of fat is the key to boosting your immune system and staying healthy. That's because certain fats provide linoleic acid, the raw material that your body needs to produce amazing microhormones called *eicosanoids*.

The body of knowledge about *eicosanoids* is a relatively new, exciting and ever expanding area of scientific research. Think of eicosanoids as master control hormones that regulate many of your

Good Series-One Eicosanoids	Bad Series-Two Eicosanoids
Enhance immunity	Suppress immunity
Decrease inflammation	Increase inflammation
Decrease pain	Increase pain
Increase oxygen flow	Decrease oxygen flow
Increase endurance	Decrease endurance
Prevent blood clotting	Promote blood clotting
Dilate airways	Constrict airways
Increase rate of cell growth	Decrease rate of cell growth

body's biological functions, including other hormones such as insulin and glucagon.

Your body manufactures two families of eicosanoids - Good eicosanoids (known as Series One) and Bad eicosanoids (Series Two).

Note: Once again, "bad" is a relative term. For example, while "bad" eicosanoids may constrict blood vessels and airways, they also promote blood clotting, which stops you from bleeding to death from a paper cut.

Leading researchers continue to explore the link between the kinds of eicosanoids the body manufactures and wellness. Evidence continues to mount that poor health and disease may be due to your body making more "bad" eicosanoids than "good" eicosanoids. In other words, the key to good health is to produce more good eicosanoids than bad eicosanoids.

Three Steps to Improve your Eicosanoid Balance

1. Eat protein-rich, favorable-carbohydrate meals. As you know, following the *Total Health* eating program stimulates the release of fat-burning glucagons and inhibits the release of fat-storing insulin. These same powerful hormones also affect the production of good and bad eicosanoids. Insulin activates delta 5 desaturase, an enzyme that promotes the production of bad eicosanoids. Glucagon, which works in opposition to insulin, inhibits this enzyme.

Excess carbohydrates also inhibit another important enzyme called delta 6 desaturase. Delta 6 desaturase allows linoleic acid - the raw material your body needs to make all eicosanoids - to enter the eicosanoid production pathway. When this enzyme is active, your body processes all the linoleic acid it needs to produce eicosanoids.

Eating more protein and less carbohydrates is the most important step you can take to restore your eicosanoid balance.

2. Eat foods that supply plenty of linoleic acid. Linoleic acid is the essential fatty acid that your body uses as building blocks for all eicosanoids. Without adequate amounts of linoleic acid, you are starving your body's ecosanoid production pipeline. The best sources for linoleic acid are olive, almond, hazelnut, safflower, light sesame, sunflower and walnut oils.

3. Stay away from trans fatty acids. Trans fatty acids are found in oils that have been altered by food manufacturers. Trans fatty acids inhibit the delta 6 desaturase enzyme and the production of good eicossnoids. They have also been linked to heart disease.

One of the most common sources of trans fatty acids is partially hydrogenated vegetable oil, the key ingredient in margarine, processed peanut butter and thousands of other products. So look for natural peanut butter (the kind with the oil on the top) and go back to putting butter on your vegetables.

Don't mistake my recommendation to use butter as a license to go wild. We still want to use foods higher in fat in moderation.

More Ways to Make Good Eicosanoids

For most people eating protein-rich, favorable-carbohydrate meals, fats rich in linoleic acid and avoiding foods loaded with trans fatty acids is enough to kick the production of good eicosanoids into high gear. But to tip the odds even more in your favor, here are three more ways to fine tune your balance of eicosanoids:

- **Avoid foods with high levels of alpha linoleic acid (ALA).** ALA is another fatty acid that suppresses good eicosanoid production by inhibiting the delta 6 desaturase enzyme. ALA is primarily found in flaxseed oil, soybean oil and canola oil. Instead, use olive oil, which has no ALA. If the distinctive taste of olive oil is a problem, another good choice is light sesame oil.

- **Watch your intake of arachadonic acid (AA).** This fatty acid is found in the fat of red meat, organ meats and egg yolks. Your body converts AA directly into bad eicosanoids. If you choose to eat red meat, trim off the fat to avoid the fat's high AA content. Instead of egg yolks, use egg whites or substitutes.

  Watching the amount of arachidonic acid you ingest is only important if you are overly sensitive to large amounts. Signs of AA sensitivity include brittle hair and nails, dry, flaking skin and minor rashes. If you are reducing excess insulin and producing more glucagons and you are not experiencing these symptoms, you probably don't have a problem with AA.

- **Eat foods rich in eicosapentanoic acid (EPA).** EPA is an essential fatty acid found in fish oil that slows the production of bad eicosanoids. Good sources of EPA include salmon, tuna, herring and fish oil capsules.

3. Why didn't my doctor tell me that fat does not make you fat or responsible for raising my cholesterol that much?

Unfortunately your doctor, just like the general public, has been misinformed by studies that are many times financed by the food industry. Also, medical schools spend very little time educating doctors on proper nutrition and prevention.

The fact that most medical doctors are not well informed on proper nutrition is really not their fault. The majority of their time in medical school is reserved for learning how to diagnose many different diseases and what types of medications or treatments to prescribe to combat those diseases. Therefore they must depend on the information they read through journals and publications outside of their normal education.

No medical doctor would disagree with the fact that proper diet and exercise is good for you. Unfortunately much of the information they've been reading about proper diet is based on studies that were financed by the food industry. The food industry has made hundreds of millions and probably into the billions of dollars off the American public with this low-fat, no-fat diet craze.

How many people do you know who have had high cholesterol and told by their physicians to cut out foods with fat? How many people do you know who have cut out the fat and actually lowered their cholesterol levels? Probably not many.

Normally physicians are so busy diagnosing and treating their patients; they don't have the time to consult on proper nutrition. That's why they refer their patients out to dieticians and nutritionists. In fact about 30-40% of my patient referrals come from medical doctors.

Unfortunately the majority of dieticians and nutritionists are still following the same misinformation of the high-carbohydrate, low-fat diet. Much of which has been promoted by the present U.S.D.A Food Guide Pyramid.

Therefore their results with most patients are poor at best and eventually the patients get frustrated and abandon all hope of gaining control of their health through diet and exercise.

By the way, the U.S.D.A. is not to blame either. The U.S.D.A.'s intentions of promoting good health through the Food Pyramid were pure. They were just misinformed along with the rest of us. Now that the truth is out, discussions are already underway among officials to *turn the food pyramid upside down.*

Several years ago before I started my *Total Health* program, I too followed the low-fat, high-carbohydrate diet. I had the unique opportunity as a doctor of chiropractic to work in a medical office with doctors who specialized in family practice. We referred a number of patients to each other. Many of our "shared" patients suffered from problems caused by obesity, such as high blood pressure, high cholesterol, and diabetes. Conditions that these patients preferred to address through lifestyle changes in diet and exercise rather than medication.

So the M.D.s recommended a low-fat, high-carbohydrate diet and exercise program, an approach that was popular at the time. But there was a problem. It wasn't working!

Even though our patients were following the classic low-fat, high-carbohydrate nutritional guidelines promoted by the healthcare community, they were not losing much weight. They were not regulating their blood sugar levels. They were not lowering cholesterol or reducing their blood pressure.

At the same time, I began to have some health problems of my own. Namely, I couldn't keep my energy levels up. I've always been a very active person. In high school, I was an All-American wrestler. And as a doctor, one of my passions was cross training for triathlons.

So I was riding my bike, swimming and running. I was also training a couple mornings a week in a form of Brazilian Jujitsu. I was taking my supplements. And I was on my high-carb, low-fat diet. When it came to training and nutrition, I was doing everything right. I figured I should be a superhuman. Instead I was exhausted.

I'd have my high-carb meal, the pasta with the low-fat red sauce and some veggies, and about half an hour later, I felt like I needed to take a nap. I knew something was wrong. I even had my blood tested for anemia.

About the same time, I became aware of nutritional principles popularized by best-selling books such as *Enter The Zone* by Barry Sears, Ph.D., and *Protein Power* by Michael Eades, M.D. and Mary Eades, M.D. According to these books, you could increase your energy levels by regulating your blood sugars.

The key was to eat protein-rich, favorable-carbohydrate meals. Not eliminating all carbohydrates, just increasing the protein and easing off the unfavorable forms of carbohydrates.

So I decided to give *The Zone* a try. For one thing, the physiology behind this way of eating made sense. For another, this was a balanced approach to eating, not some extreme alternative like diet pills or liquid meals.

The results were fantastic. Within about two weeks my energy levels soared. I also lost about five pounds around the middle. Remember, all I wanted was more energy. The weight loss was a bonus! Most of all, I was excited about the prospect of sharing this information with my patients.

But unfortunately, I couldn't tell my patients to go out and buy these books because they were too technical for most people to understand. So I did more research, and used my personal experience to make this exciting information accessible and easy to use in the real world.

The dramatic results I began to see in my patients were nothing short of life changing. Patients who were obese have lost the weight. In many cases, their M.D.s have taken them off their high blood pressure medications, their diabetes medications and their cholesterol medications. And the weight has stayed off. *Total Health* is not some fad diet. It's a way of eating that will work for the rest of your life.

Remember, it's not the fat you eat that raises your cholesterol, blood pressure or blood sugars. It's the excess insulin from all of those carbohydrates you've been eating. The following are actual blood tests from one of my patients.

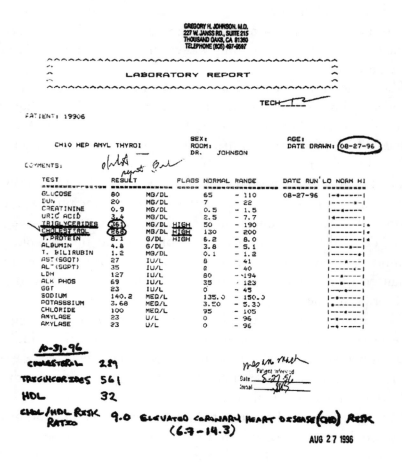

Blood Test #1: Before *Total Health*

The first one was done through his M.D. It showed a triglyceride level at 361, twice the high end of normal, which is between 50 and 190. Cholesterol was at 268. Normal is at 130 to 200 (see Blood Test #1)

Obviously, his physician was quite alarmed, so he ran another blood test a couple months later. Now his cholesterol was at 289; triglycerides were up to 561. His HDLs were at 32, and his cholesterol to high density lipid risk ratio was at 9.0. That's well into the elevated coronary heart disease risk category. In other words, he was a heart attack waiting to happen. And he was just 44 years old. Oh, by the way, the *coronary heart disease risk ratio* is the key to how we were all deceived by the original studies on fat and cholesterol over 20 years ago!

The *coronary heart disease risk ratio* is the true determining factor as to whether or not you're more pre-disposed to coronary heart disease and a future heart attack. Many times your cholesterol can be elevated, but if your cholesterol to HDL (high density lipids) risk ratio is low you're fine. When your HDLs or good lipids are higher, they'll offset the ill effects of slightly elevated cholesterol levels.

Many of the studies on fat, which have been financed by the food industry over the years, conveniently failed to tell us about the *coronary heart disease risk ratio*. The original studies took two groups of people- one group who ate a lot of fat-and the group who ate very little fat. The group that ate a lot of fat had higher cholesterol levels, but the cholesterol to high density lipid risk ratios were virtually the same in both groups.

After seven weeks on the *Total Health* program, my patient had dropped 30 pounds. His cholesterol went from 289 to 174, which is within the normal range. His triglycerides went from 561 down to 107, which is smack in the middle of normal. His cholesterol to HDL or his coronary heart disease risk ratio went from 9.0 to 3.7, which is below average risk.

This was with no medications! I literally have hundreds of pre and post blood tests of patients showing equal or even better results!

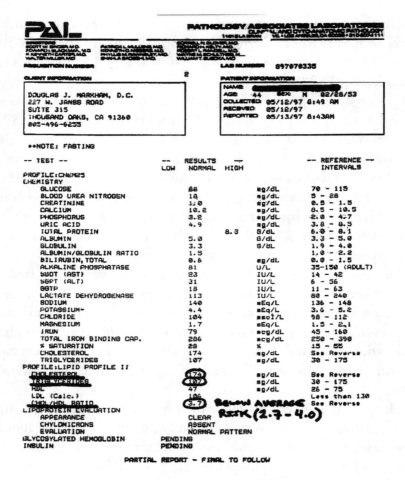

Blood Test #2: After *Total Health*

How to use Food to Help your Medical Doctor Potentially Reduce or Discontinue Your Medications for High Blood Pressure, High Cholesterol and Adult-Onset Diabetes

Caution: Never reduce or discontinue prescription medications without the consent and direction of your physician!

The above blood test results are objective proof of *how to use food to help your medical doctor potentially reduce or discontinue your medications for high blood pressure, high cholesterol and adult-onset diabetes.*

The key to preventing yourself from the need for prescription medications, the potential reduction or discontinued use of medications related to high blood pressure, high cholesterol and adult-onset diabetes is blood sugar regulation.

Whether you're suffering from excess weight gain leading to high blood pressure, high cholesterol from your own liver cells producing excess cholesterol, or your cells are developing a resistance to insulin, the culprit is excess carbohydrate consumption leading to elevated blood sugars! This is discussed in more detail in the previous section of *The Dangers of Excess Insulin*.

Once you start following the *Total Health* protein-rich, favorable-carbohydrate way of eating, you'll start to realize the benefits of controlled blood sugars. The excess weight will start coming off, your sustained energy levels will start to increase, your cholesterol will begin lowering, blood pressure will start lowering and your blood sugar will drop.

Therefore, if you're taking medications to lower your cholesterol, your blood pressure or oral medications for the beginning stages of adult-onset diabetes, you should be able to go back to your medical doctor to have them start monitoring your progress and begin lowering your medications.

In many cases, like with hundreds of my own patients, your medical doctor will be able to completely eliminate your medications for high blood pressure, high cholesterol and adult-onset diabetes.

Note: If you're taking blood sugar medications, it's very important that you are monitoring your blood sugars on a daily basis. This is because as your blood sugars start to lower naturally, the blood sugar lowering medications will drive your blood sugars down even further. This can lead to light headedness, etc. as a result of excessively low blood sugars. You must consult with your medical doctor immediately, so they can start reducing your blood sugar lowering medications. The same holds true with blood pressure medications.

*__**Always consult with your physician before beginning any kind of changes in your diet or medications!__ **__*

4. Much of what has been written about the nutritional principles behind eating a diet with more protein and less carbohydrates is too technical, not totally effective, or not well balanced.

Dr. Sears did a great job of verifying the scientific basis of how and why a protein-rich, favorable-carbohydrate way of eating is healthier and much more effective than the classic low-fat, high-carbohydrate diet in his book *Enter The Zone*. Unfortunately the information in the book was too technical for many readers to understand and implement into their lives.

The other problem is that Dr. Sears is a research scientist and never actually had his own weight loss/wellness clinic. His program is based on the 40-30-30 concept. This represents the amount of carbohydrates, protein, and fat someone should eat at each meal or snack. He suggests 40% carbohydrates, 30% protein, and 30% fat.

What I have observed with patients who have come to my office following the Zone program is that they usually lose some weight and feel better, but they often do not reach their target weight loss goals. They may lose 20 or 30 pounds and still have 10-20 more pounds to go. This leads to frustration and many times they will abandon the program. The reason for this plateau in weight loss is due to not limiting their carbohydrate intake enough to get the job done.

The Atkins plan on the other hand suggests limiting your carbohydrate intake a lot more in his book *Dr. Atkins' New Diet Revolution*. This is good for rapid weight loss, but many healthcare providers feel it can be too rapid. Burning fat too fast can lead to a condition called *ketosis*. The byproduct of burning fat is *ketones*, which accumulate in the body and pass through our kidneys before being excreted in the urine. This is thought to be potentially damaging to the kidneys.

The Atkins plan also suggests eliminating fruits as a carbohydrate choice from your diet during the induction phase of the program. This suggestion, along with allowing people to disregard the amount of daily fat intake, leads to skepticism of an unbalanced approach to weight loss and health. This is where I'm in agreement with the nutritional establishment. I still want people to choose healthier fat options and don't want them to disregard the fat content of meals.

I also allow fiber-rich fruits in the weight loss stages as long as they are on the low-glycemic *Food Unit List* in the **Eating Your Way to Health** section of this book. Fruits are healthier carbohydrate choices containing essential nutrient value and will not inhibit weight loss as long as they're not consumed in excessive amounts.

The other point that separates the *Total Health* plan from the Atkin's plan is portion control. We need to base the amount of protein we eat at each meal on the size of our body frames. This is called your *Daily Protein Requirement*. This will also be outlined in the **Eating Your Way to Health** section.

The new approach to the subject of a higher protein, lower carbohydrate diet that separates *Total Health* from other plans like *The Zone* and *Dr. Atkins' New Diet Revolution* is that it's an easier, more effective, safer, clinically-proven way to burn fat, stay healthy and boost your energy.

Total Health achieves this through promoting a healthy balance of quality protein choices and carbohydrates in the form of fiber-rich fruits and vegetables.

Total Health also offers a more effective follow-up program for its readers by offering a free one-month subscription of customized weight loss and wellness menu options online at **www.totalhealthdoc.com**.

5. The key to any weight loss and wellness program is accountability and proper follow-up. After several thousand in-office weight loss and wellness consultations, the patients who have the best results are those who have committed to weekly follow-up visits.

When I first started writing *Total Health* I struggled with how to offer my readers the same customized weight loss and wellness menu options that I give to my patients. The other dilemma was offering the same kind of effective accountability and proper follow-up that my patients received on a weekly basis. The only answer was to write a book that gave people a simple way to understand why they should follow a protein-rich, favorable-carbohydrate way of eating and give them a more effective way to properly follow through with their weight loss and wellness goals.

I didn't want my book to be like all of the others collecting dust up on a shelf because it was too technical or full of generic diets and menus that most people could not implement into their daily lives. Therefore I created www.totalhealthdoc.com to help people take control of their health using the same clinically-proven principles and customized menus that have worked on thousands of my own patients.

- All menus and food choices are customized for your body size, weight loss and health goals.
- Easy-to-follow food options for breakfast, lunch, dinner, and snacks make it easy to know what to eat and when.
- An extensive list of everyday protein-rich, favorable-carbohydrate foods offer variety and flexibility.
- Over 120 different protein-rich, favorable-carbohydrate recipes.
- Food preparation tips for dining out in *Total Health*.
- Convenient "fast-food" options for drive-thru dining.
- *Total Health* success tips to speed your progress.
- Personalized weight loss and wellness guidance via e-mail.

Dieters who received personalized weight loss guidance via e-mail shed more pounds than those who didn't get extra help, according to an updated study by researchers at the Brown University School of Medicine in Providence.

Visit **www.totalhealthdoc.com** for personalized weight loss and wellness guidance.

Part II

Eating Your Way To Health

Pulling It All Together

Okay, we've talked about the connection between the food you eat, your blood sugar levels and the hormonal response to burn or store body fat. How does this work in the real world?

Whether your goal is to reduce body fat, increase mental and physical productivity or reduce your chances of illness, the *Total Health* protein-rich, favorable-carbohydrate way of eating is for you. To get started on a protein-rich, favorable-carbohydrate way of eating, the first thing you have to do is figure out your *daily protein requirement*. In other words, how much protein your body needs on a daily basis. Remember, the *Total Health* plan is not a "high-protein" diet. It's a healthy way of eating based on your body's daily protein needs.

Your *daily protein requirement* is determined by your percentage of *lean body mass* multiplied by your ideal percentage body fat. Lean body mass refers to the percentage of your body that isn't fat. This is basically your bone and muscle weight. The fastest and most accurate way to determine your *lean body mass* is to use an electrical impedance body fat analyzer.

The following chart reflects your *ideal body fat percentage* based on your age and gender:

Ideal Body Fat Percentages

AGE	MALES	FEMALES
10 - 30	12% - 18%	20% - 26%
31 - 40	13% - 19%	21% - 27%
41 - 50	14% - 20%	22% - 28%
51 - 60	16% - 20%	22% - 30%
61 & Above	17% - 21%	22% - 31%

The way we determine your *lean body mass* is to subtract your *fat pounds* from your *total body weight*. So if you weighed 150 pounds and you had 50 pounds of fat, your *lean body mass* (fat-free body weight), would be 100 pounds.

Determining Your Ideal Weight

To calculate your *ideal weight*, simply multiply your *lean body mass* by your *ideal percentage body fat* and add the total to your *lean body mass*. So, if you were a 25 year-old female with 100 pounds of *lean body mass* and wanted to reach the high-end of *ideal percentage body fat* of 26%, your ideal weight would be 126 pounds.

Calculating Your Daily Protein Requirement

Once we've determined your *lean body mass*, we multiply your *lean body mass* by your *daily activity index*. This means how active you are, which is anything from 0.5, which is "couch potato" material, to 0.9 which is someone who exercises daily.

The Activity Levels:
1. **Sedentary** - no physical activity; protein need is 0.5 grams per pound of *lean body mass*.
2. **Moderately Active** - 20-30 minutes of exercise, 2-3 times per week; protein need is 0.6 grams per pound of *lean body mass*.
3. **Active** - 30 minutes of exercise, 3-5 times per week; protein need is 0.7 grams per pound of *lean body mass*.
4. **Very Active** - vigorous exercise activity over an hour or more 5 or more times per week; protein need is 0.8 grams per pound of *lean body mass*.

5. **Athlete** - athlete in training, twice-daily heavy workouts for an hour or more; protein need is <u>0.9 grams</u> per pound of *lean body mass*.

So, if your *lean body mass* was 100 pounds and you were in the *active* category of activity levels, you would multiply 0.7 times 100 for a *daily protein requirement* of 70 grams of protein per day.

A Simple Alternative to Calculating Your Daily Protein Requirement

If you're confused about the previous information and don't have access to a body fat analyzer, we have provided the following choices for your approximate *daily protein requirement* according to your body frame size:

Petite Body Frame .... (60-70 grams of protein per day)
Small Body Frame .... (70-80 grams of protein per day)
Medium Body Frame .. (80-90 grams of protein per day)
Large Body Frame .... (90-100 grams of protein per day)

*If you exercise 3 times per week or more, add 10 grams of protein per day.

To determine your body frame size, place yourself into the following body frame category according to your height:

Petite Body Frame: ...... 5 feet 1 inches and below
Small Body Frame: ...... 5 feet 2 inches to 5 feet 5 inches
Medium Body Frame: . 5 feet 6 inches to 5 feet 9 inches
Large Body Frame: ...... 5 feet 10 inches and above

Simply match your body frame size with the following appropriate *Total Health Protein-Rich, Favorable-Carbohydrate Prepared Meal Menu Options.*

Total Health Protein-Rich, Favorable-Carbohydrate Prepared Meal Menu Options

PETITE BODY FRAME (60-70 GRAMS OF PROTEIN PER DAY)
MODERATE WEIGHT LOSS (40 GRAMS OF CARBHYDRATE PER DAY)

BREAKFAST 8:00 A.M.
14 GRAMS PROTEIN
10 GRAMS CARBOHYDRATE

OPTION #1
Protein
1/2 cup of low fat (2%) *or* no fat cottage cheese
Carbohydrate
Favorite Fruit- Choose 1 unit (9 carbohydrate grams) of your favorite fruit choice listed on the **Macronutrient Food Unit List.**

OPTION #2
Protein
Omelette (2 egg whites or 1/4 cup of egg substitute) with: **1 oz. cheese** or **1 oz. meat.** (If you do not want meat, substitute an extra egg white, 1/4 cup of egg substitute or 1oz. cheese.) *You may add mushrooms, onions, salsa, avocado, etc. without having to count them as part of your carbohydrate intake.
Carbohydrate
Favorite Fruit- Choose 1 unit (9 carbohydrate grams) of your favorite fruit choice listed on the **Macronutrient Food Unit List** or 1 tomato or 1/3 bagel or 1/2 English muffin or 1 low carbohydrate tortilla or 1 slice toast (low carbohydrate brand).
*Note: See **www.lowcarboptions.com** for low carbohydrate bread and tortilla brand recommendations.*

OPTION #3
Protein
2 **Cheese Sticks** (string cheese) *or* 2 oz. cheese *or* 2 oz. meat *or* 2 oz. turkey or beef jerky

Carbohydrate

Favorite Fruit- Choose 1 unit (9 carbohydrate grams) of your favorite fruit choice listed on the **Macronutrient Food Unit List.**

OPTION #4

Protein

1 **Cheese Stick** (string cheese) *or* 1 **oz. cheese** *or* 1 **oz. meat** *or* 1 oz. turkey or beef jerky

Carbohydrate and Protein

1/2 40-30-30 Protein Bar *or* 1 Protein Bar without adding cheese if protein to carbohydrate ratios are adequate.

*Note: See **www.lowcarboptions.com** for protein bar brand recommendations.*

OPTION #5

Protein

2 **Cheese Sticks** (string cheese) *or* 2 **oz. cheese** *or* 2 **oz. meat** *or* 2 **oz. turkey or beef jerky** *or* 1 scoop Protein Powder

Carbohydrate and Protein

1/4 cup **Light Yogurt** - any flavor *or* 1/2 cup plain yogurt

OPTION #6 (Fast Food Option)

Breakfast Sandwich: 1 Egg and cheese or meat (w/out top muffin or bun)

Breakfast Burrito: 1 Egg and cheese burrito (tear-off 1/2 tortilla)

OPTION #7

1/3 bagel *or* 1/2 English muffin *or* 1 slice toast with 2 oz. cream cheese and/or lox *or* 1 Tbsp. natural peanut *or* nut butter with 1 cheese stick *or* 1 oz. cheese *or* 1 oz. meat

OPTION #8

1/3 cup of oatmeal with 1 scoop protein powder *or* omelette

OPTION #9

1 **Protein meal replacement shake** (add protein powder to milk or water)

*Note: See **www.lowcarboptions.com** for protein powder brand recommendations.*

LUNCH 12:00 NOON AND DINNER 7:00 P.M.
14 GRAMS PROTEIN
10 GRAMS CARBOHYDRATE

OPTION #1
Protein
Chicken (2-3 oz.), Beef (2-3 oz.), Pork (2-3 oz.), Fish (3-4 oz.) *or* favorite **protein** choice found on the **Macronutrient Food Unit List.** You may add approximately 1 tablespoon of your favorite sauce (barbecue, teriyaki, etc.) and your favorite spices.
Note: Vegetarian protein choices are found on the Macronutrient Food Unit List.

Carbohydrate
Favorite Vegetables and/or **Green Salad**- Choose 1 unit (9 carbohydrate grams) of your favorite vegetable choices listed on the **Macronutrient Food Unit List.** You may combine several different vegetable choices together as long as the total grams of carbohydrate adds up to 1 unit (9 grams). Example: 1 cup of cauliflower and 1/2 cup of broccoli.
Note: See Food Preparation Tips for butter and salad dressing application recommendations.

OPTION #2
Protein
Tuna (3-4 oz.) *or* Chicken (3-4 oz.) salad (with mayonnaise) *or* Deli meat (3-4 oz.)
Carbohydrate
1 tomato or 1 avocado (medium size) or 1/3 bagel or 1/2 English muffin or 1 low carbohydrate tortilla or 1 slice toast (low carbohydrate brand). You may add mayonnaise and mustard to taste.
Note: See www.lowcarboptions.com for low carbohydrate bread and tortilla brand recommendations.

OPTION #3 (Fast Food Options)

Garden Fresh Salads: 1 salad with choice of favorite protein (with favorite dressing, no croutons)

Chicken *or* Steak Burrito: 1 burrito (no tortilla or tear-off 1/2 of tortilla w/out rice and beans). Guacamole, salsa and sour cream are fine in conservative amounts.

Chicken *or* Steak Soft Taco: 1 soft taco (tear-off 1/2 of tortilla)

Deli-Style *or* Sub-Sandwich: 1 sandwich with preferred choice of meat or cheese (w/out top bun or protein style-wrapped in lettuce)

Grilled Chicken Sandwich: 1 grilled chicken sandwich (w/out top bun or protein style-wrapped in lettuce)

Rotisserie *or* Grilled Chicken: 1 skinless thigh, leg, or breast with 1 side cole slaw

Hamburger: 1 hamburger or cheeseburger (w/out top bun or protein style-wrapped in lettuce)

Pizza: 2 slices (eat toppings only - cheese, meat, etc.)

Note: You will maintain a low-fat diet naturally by selecting your protein choices from the Best Choice categories in the Macronutrient Food Unit List.

SNACK 3:30 and (11:00 P.M. - Optional)
7 GRAMS PROTEIN
5 GRAMS CARBOHYDRATE

OPTION #1
1 celery stalk filled with 1 tablespoon of natural peanut *or* nut butter *or* 2 oz. cream cheese

OPTION #2
1 cheese stick (string cheese) or **1oz. cheese *or* 1oz. meat** with favorite fruit- choose1/2 unit (4.5 carbohydrate grams) of your favorite fruit choice listed on the **Macronutrient Food Unit List.**

OPTION #3
1/4 cup of nuts (any type)

OPTION #4

Hot *or* Iced cafe latte (1% milk) coffee drink (sugar-free)- Ask the coffee establishment to add a shot of flavored "sugar-free" syrup if available. You may also ask them to blend your iced cafe latte in the blender with the added "sugar-free" syrup for a "sugar-free" ice blended coffee drink. Some coffee establishments have prepared "sugar-free" ice blended coffee drinks.

*Note: See **www.lowcarboptions.com** for sugar-free syrup brand recommendations.*

OPTION #5

1 4-6 oz. glass of milk (skim, 1%, or 2%)

OPTION #6

1/2 cup Light Yogurt - any flavor *or* 1/2 cup of plain yogurt

OPTION #7

1/2 40-30-30 *or* Protein Bar (any flavor)

OPTION #8

1 4-6 oz. glass of wine (dry red or dry white) *or* light-beer with 1 cheese stick (string cheese) *or* 1 oz. cheese *or* 1 oz. meat *or* 1 oz. turkey or beef jerky

OPTION #9

1 deviled *or* hard boiled egg

OPTION #10

1/4 cup ice cream (any brand or flavor) with 1 oz. cheese

NOTE: FREE SNACKS: You may eat certain sugar-free chocolate bars, candies, Jello or pork skins anytime without having to count them as a snack. You may also put a squirt of real whipped cream on the Jello.

Homemade sugar-free popsicles are also an acceptable free snack. Use a popsicle mold and add your favorite sugar-free soda, etc.

*Note: See **www.lowcarboptions.com** for sugar-free chocolate bar and candy brand recommendations.*

SMALL BODY FRAME (70-80 GRAMS OF PROTEIN PER DAY)
MODERATE WEIGHT LOSS (40 GRAMS OF CARBHYDRATE PER DAY)

BREAKFAST 8:00 A.M.
21 GRAMS PROTEIN
10 GRAMS CARBOHYDRATE

OPTION #1:
  Protein
  3/4 cup of low fat (2%) *or* no fat cottage cheese
  Carbohydrate
  Favorite Fruit- Choose 1 unit (9 carbohydrate grams) of your favorite fruit choice listed on the **Macronutrient Food Unit List.**

OPTION #2
  Protein
  Omelette (2 egg whites or 1/4 cup of egg substitute) with: **1 oz. cheese *and* 1 oz. meat.** (If you do not want meat, substitute an extra egg white, 1/4 cup of egg substitute or 1oz. cheese.) *You may add mushrooms, onions, salsa, avocado, etc. without having to count them as part of your carbohydrate intake.
  Carbohydrate
  Favorite Fruit- Choose 1 unit (9 carbohydrate grams) of your favorite fruit choice listed on the **Macronutrient Food Unit List** or 1 tomato or 1/3 bagel or 1/2 English muffin or 1 low carbohydrate tortilla or 1 slice toast (low carbohydrate brand).
  *Note: See **www.lowcarboptions.com** for low carbohydrate bread and tortilla brand recommendations.*

OPTION #3
  Protein
  3 Cheese Sticks (string cheese) *or* 3 oz. cheese *or* 3 oz. meat *or* 3 oz. turkey or beef jerky
  Carbohydrate
  Favorite Fruit- Choose 1 unit (9 carbohydrate grams) of your favorite fruit choice listed on the **Macronutrient Food Unit List.**

OPTION #4

Protein

2 Cheese Sticks (string cheese) *or* 2 oz. cheese *or* 2 oz. meat *or* 2 oz. turkey or beef jerky

Carbohydrate and Protein

1/2 40-30-30 Bar *or* 1 Protein Bar without adding cheese if protein to carbohydrate ratios are adequate.

*Note: See **www.lowcarboptions.com** for protein bar brand recommendations.*

OPTION #5

Protein

3 Cheese Sticks (string cheese) *or* 3 oz. cheese *or* 3 oz. meat *or* 3 oz. turkey or beef jerky *or* 1 scoop Protein Powder

Carbohydrate and Protein

1/4 cup Light Yogurt - any flavor *or* 1/2 cup plain yogurt

OPTION #6 (Fast Food Option)

Breakfast Sandwich: 1 Egg, cheese and meat (w/out top muffin or bun)

Breakfast Burrito: 1 Egg and cheese burrito (tear-off 1/2 tortilla)

OPTION #7

1/3 bagel or 1/2 English muffin or 1 slice toast with 3 oz. cream cheese and/or lox *or* 1 Tbsp. natural peanut or nut butter with 2 cheese sticks *or* 2 oz. cheese *or* 2 oz. meat

OPTION #8

1/3 cup of oatmeal with 1 scoop protein powder *or* omelette

OPTION #9

1 Protein meal replacement shake (add protein powder to milk or water)

*Note: See **www.lowcarboptions.com** for protein powder brand recommendations.*

LUNCH 12:00 NOON AND DINNER 7:00 P.M.
21 GRAMS PROTEIN
10 GRAMS CARBOHYDRATE

OPTION #1
Protein
Chicken (3-4 oz.), Beef (3-4 oz.), Pork (3-4 oz.), Fish (4.5 oz.)
or **favorite protein choice** found on the **Macronutrient Food
Unit List.** You may add approximately 1 tablespoon of your
favorite sauce (barbecue, teriyaki, etc.) and your favorite spices.
*Note: Vegetarian protein choices are found on the **Macronutrient
Food Unit List.***

Carbohydrate
Favorite Vegetables and/or **Green Salad**- Choose 1 unit (9
carbohydrate grams) of your favorite vegetable choices listed on
the **Macronutrient Food Unit List.** You may combine several
differentvegetable choices together as long as the total grams of
carbohydrate adds up to 1 unit (9 grams). Example: 1 cup of
cauliflower and 1/2 cup of broccoli.
*Note: See **Food Preparation Tips** for butter and salad dressing
application recommendations.*

OPTION #2
Protein
Tuna (3-4 oz.) *or* Chicken (3-4 oz.) **salad** (with mayonnaise) *or*
Deli meat (3-4 oz.)
Carbohydrate
1 tomato or 1 avocado (medium size) or 1/3 bagel or 1/2 English
muffin or 1 low carbohydrate tortilla or 1 slice toast (low carbohydrate
brand). You may add mayonnaise and mustard to taste.
*Note: See **www.lowcarboptions.com** for low carbohydrate bread
and tortilla brand recommendations.*

OPTION #3 (Fast Food Options)
Garden Fresh Salads: 1 salad with choice of favorite protein (with
favorite dressing, no croutons)

Chicken or Steak Burrito: 1 burrito (no tortilla or tear-off 1/2 of tortilla w/out rice and beans). Guacamole, salsa and sour cream are fine in conservative amounts.

Chicken or Steak Soft Taco: 1 soft taco (tear-off 1/2 of tortilla)

Deli-Style or Sub-Sandwich: 1 sandwich with preferred choice of meat or cheese (w/out top bun or protein style-wrapped in lettuce)

Grilled Chicken Sandwich: 1 grilled chicken sandwich (w/out top bun or protein style-wrapped in lettuce)

Rotisserie or Grilled Chicken: 1 skinless thigh, leg, or breast with 1 side cole slaw

Hamburger: 1 hamburger or cheeseburger (w/out top bun or protein style-wrapped in lettuce)

Pizza: 2 slices (eat toppings only - cheese, meat, etc.)

Note: You will maintain a low-fat diet naturally by selecting your protein choices from the Best Choice categories on the Macronutrient Food Unit List.

SNACK 3:30 and (11:00 P.M. - Optional)
7 GRAMS PROTEIN
5 GRAMS CARBOHYDRATE

OPTION #1
1 celery stalk filled with 1 tablespoon of natural peanut or nut butter *or* 2 oz. cream cheese

OPTION #2
1 cheese stick (string cheese) **or 1 oz. cheese** *or* 1 oz. meat with favorite fruit-choose1/2 unit (4.5 carbohydrate grams) of your *favorite fruit choice* listed on the **Macronutrient Food Unit List.**

OPTION #3
1/4 cup of nuts (any type)

OPTION #4

Hot or Iced cafe latte (1% milk) coffee drink (sugar-free)- Ask the coffee establishment to add a shot of flavored "sugar-free" syrup if available. You may also ask them to blend your iced cafe latte in the blender with the added "sugar-free" syrup for a "sugar-free" ice blended coffee drink. Some coffee establishments have prepared "sugar-free" ice blended coffee drinks.
Note: See **www.lowcarboptions.com** for sugar-free syrup brand recommendations.

OPTION #5

1 4-6 oz. glass of milk (skim, 1%, or 2%)

OPTION #6

1/2 cup Light Yogurt - any flavor or 1/2 cup of plain yogurt

OPTION #7

1/2 40-30-30 Bar or Protein Bar

OPTION #8

1 4-6 oz. glass of wine (dry red or dry white) or light-beer with 1 cheese stick (string cheese) *or* 1 oz. cheese *or* 1 oz. meat *or* 1 oz. turkey or beef jerky

OPTION #9

1 deviled or hard boiled egg

OPTION #10

1/4 cup ice cream (any brand or flavor) with 1 oz. cheese

NOTE: FREE SNACKS: You may eat certain sugar-free chocolate bars, candies, Jello or pork skins anytime without having to count them as a snack. You may also put a squirt of real whipped cream on the Jello.

Homemade sugar-free popsicles are also an acceptable free snack. Use a popsicle mold and add your favorite sugar-free soda, etc.

*Note: See **www.lowcarboptions.com** for sugar-free chocolate bar and candy brand recommendations.*

BREAKFAST 8:00 A.M.
21 GRAMS PROTEIN
10 GRAMS CARBOHYDRATE

OPTION #1:
Protein
3/4 cup of low fat (2%) **or no fat cottage cheese**
Carbohydrate
Favorite Fruit- Choose 1 unit (9 carbohydrate grams) of your favorite fruit choice listed on the **Macronutrient Food Unit List.**

OPTION #2
Protein
Omelette (2 egg whites or 1/4 cup of egg substitute) with: **1 oz. cheese and 1 oz.meat.** (If you do not want meat, substitute an extra egg white, 1/4 cup of egg substitute or 1oz. cheese.) *You may add mushrooms, onions, salsa, avocado, etc. without having to count them as part of your carbohydrate intake.
Carbohydrate
Favorite Fruit- Choose 1 unit (9 carbohydrate grams) of your favorite fruit choice listed on the **Macronutrient Food Unit List** or 1 tomato or 1/3 bagel or 1/2 English muffin or 1 low carbohydrate tortilla or 1 slice toast (low carbohydrate brand).
*Note: See **www.lowcarboptions.com** for low carbohydrate bread and tortilla brand recommendations.*

OPTION #3
Protein
3 Cheese Sticks (string cheese) *or* 3 oz. cheese *or* 3 oz. meat *or* 3 oz. turkey or beef jerky
Carbohydrate
Favorite Fruit- Choose 1 unit (9 carbohydrate grams) of your favorite fruit choice listed on the **Macronutrient Food Unit List.**

OPTION #4

Protein

2 Cheese Sticks (string cheese) *or* 2 oz. cheese *or* 2 oz. meat *or* 2 oz. turkey or beef jerky

Carbohydrate and Protein

1/2 40-30-30 Bar *or* 1 Protein Bar without adding cheese if protein to carbohydrate ratios are adequate.

*Note: See **www.lowcarboptions.com** for protein bar brand recommendations.*

OPTION #5

Protein

3 Cheese Sticks (string cheese) *or* 3 oz. cheese *or* 3 oz. meat *or* 3 oz. turkey or beef jerky *or* 1 scoop Protein Powder

Carbohydrate and Protein

1/4 cup Light Yogurt - any flavor or 1/2 cup plain yogurt

OPTION #6 (Fast Food Option)

Breakfast Sandwich: 1 Egg, cheese and meat (w/out top muffin or bun)

Breakfast Burrito: 1 Egg and cheese burrito (tear-off 1/2 tortilla)

OPTION #7

1/3 bagel or 1/2 English muffin or 1 slice toast with 3 oz. cream cheese and/or lox or 1 Tbsp. natural peanut or nut butter with 2 cheese sticks *or* 2 oz. cheese *or* 2 oz. meat

OPTION #8

1/3 cup of oatmeal with 1 scoop protein powder *or* omelette

OPTION #9

1 Protein meal replacement shake (add protein powder to milk or water)

*Note: See **www.lowcarboptions.com** for protein powder brand recommendations.*

LUNCH 12:00 NOON AND DINNER 7:00 P.M.
21 GRAMS PROTEIN
10 GRAMS CARBOHYDRATE

OPTION #1
Protein
Chicken (3-4 oz.), Beef (3-4 oz.), Pork (3-4 oz.), Fish (4.5 oz.) *or* **favorite protein choice** found on the **Macronutrient Food Unit List.** You may add approximately 1 tablespoon of your favorite sauce (barbecue, teriyaki, etc.) and your favorite spices.
*Note: Vegetarian protein choices are found on the **Macronutrient Food Unit List.***

Carbohydrate
Favorite Vegetables and/or **Green Salad**- Choose 1 unit (9 carbohydrate grams) of your favorite vegetable choices listed on the **Macronutrient Food Unit List.** You may combine several differentvegetable choices together as long as the total grams of carbohydrate adds up to 1 unit (9 grams). Example: 1 cup of cauliflower and 1/2 cup of broccoli.
*Note: See **Food Preparation Tips** for butter and salad dressing application recommendations.*

OPTION #2
Protein
Tuna (3-4 oz.) *or* Chicken (3-4 oz.) **salad** (with mayonnaise) *or* Deli meat (3-4 oz.)
Carbohydrate
1 tomato or 1 avocado (medium size) or 1/3 bagel or 1/2 English muffin or 1 low carbohydrate tortilla or 1 slice toast (low carbohydrate brand). You may add mayonnaise and mustard to taste.
*Note: See **www.lowcarboptions.com** for low carbohydrate bread and tortilla brand recommendations.*

OPTION #3 (Fast Food Options)
Garden Fresh Salads: 1 salad with choice of favorite protein (with favorite dressing, no croutons)

Chicken or Steak Burrito: 1 burrito (no tortilla or tear-off 1/2 of tortilla w/out rice and beans). Guacamole, salsa and sour cream are fine in conservative amounts.

Chicken or Steak Soft Taco: 1 soft taco (tear-off 1/2 of tortilla)

Deli-Style or Sub-Sandwich: 1 sandwich with preferred choice of meat or cheese (w/out top bun or protein style-wrapped in lettuce)

Grilled Chicken Sandwich: 1 grilled chicken sandwich (w/out top bun or protein style-wrapped in lettuce)

Rotisserie or Grilled Chicken: 1 skinless thigh, leg, or breast with 1 side cole slaw

Hamburger: 1 hamburger or cheeseburger (w/out top bun or protein style-wrapped in lettuce)

Pizza: 2 slices (eat toppings only - cheese, meat, etc.)

Note: You will maintain a low-fat diet naturally by selecting your protein choices from the Best Choice categories on the Macronutrient Food Unit List.

SNACK 3:30 and (11:00 P.M. - Optional)
7 GRAMS PROTEIN
5 GRAMS CARBOHYDRATE

OPTION #1
1 celery stalk filled with 1 tablespoon of natural peanut or nut butter *or* 2 oz. cream cheese

OPTION #2
1 cheese stick (string cheese) *or* 1oz. cheese *or* 1oz. meat with favorite fruit- choose1/2 unit (4.5 carbohydrate grams) of your **favorite fruit choice** listed on the **Macronutrient Food Unit List.**

OPTION #3
1/4 cup of nuts (any type)

OPTION #4
Hot or Iced cafe latte (1% milk) coffee drink (sugar-free)- Ask the coffee establishment to add a shot of flavored "sugar-free" syrup if available. You may also ask them to blend your iced cafe latte in the blender with the added "sugar-free" syrup for a "sugar-free" ice blended coffee drink. Some coffee establishments have prepared "sugar-free" ice blended coffee drinks.

*Note: See **www.lowcarboptions.com** for sugar-free syrup brand recommendations.*

OPTION #5
1 4-6 oz. glass of milk (skim, 1%, or 2%)

OPTION #6
1/2 cup Light Yogurt - any flavor *or* **1/2 cup of plain yogurt**

OPTION #7
1/2 40-30-30 Bar or Protein Bar

OPTION #8
1 4-6 oz. glass of wine (dry red or dry white) *or* **light-beer with 1 cheese stick** (string cheese) *or* **1 oz. cheese** *or* **1 oz. meat** *or* **1 oz. turkey or beef jerky**

OPTION #9
1 deviled or hard boiled egg

OPTION #10
1/4 cup ice cream (any brand or flavor) with 1 oz. cheese

NOTE: FREE SNACKS: **You may eat certain sugar-free chocolate bars, candies, Jello or pork skins anytime without having to count them as a snack. You may also put a squirt of real whipped cream on the Jello.**

Homemade sugar-free popsicles are also an acceptable free snack. Use a popsicle mold and add your favorite sugar-free soda, etc.

*Note: See **www.lowcarboptions.com** for sugar-free chocolate bar and candy brand recommendations.*

LARGE BODY FRAME (90-100 GRAMS OF PROTEIN PER DAY)
MODERATE WEIGHT LOSS (40 GRAMS OF CARBHYDRATE PER DAY)

BREAKFAST 8:00 A.M.
28 GRAMS PROTEIN
10 GRAMS CARBOHYDRATE

OPTION #1:
Protein
1 cup of low fat (2%) or no fat cottage cheese
Carbohydrate
Favorite Fruit- Choose 1 unit (9 carbohydrate grams) of your
favorite fruit choice listed on the **Macronutrient Food Unit List.**

OPTION #2
Protein
Omelette (2-3 egg whites or 1/2 cup of egg substitute) with: **1-
2 oz. cheese and 1 oz. meat.** (If you do not want meat, substitute
an extra egg white, 1/4 cup of egg substitute or 1oz. cheese.)
*You may add mushrooms, onions, salsa, avocado, etc. without
having to count them as part of your carbohydrate intake.*
Carbohydrate
Favorite Fruit- Choose 1 unit (9 carbohydrate grams) of your
favorite fruit choice listed on the **Macronutrient Food Unit List**
or 1 tomato or 1/3 bagel or 1/2 English muffin or 1 low
carbohydrate tortilla or 1 slice toast (low carbohydrate brand).
*Note: See **www.lowcarboptions.com** for low carbohydrate bread
and tortilla brand recommendations.*

OPTION #3
Protein
4 Cheese Sticks (string cheese) *or* **4 oz. cheese** *or* **3 oz. meat** *or*
r **4 oz. turkey or beef jerky**
Carbohydrate
Favorite Fruit- Choose 1 unit (9 carbohydrate grams) of your
favorite fruit choice listed on the **Macronutrient Food Unit List.**

OPTION #4
Protein
3 Cheese Sticks (string cheese) *or* 3 oz. cheese *or* 3 oz. meat *or* 3 oz. turkey or beef jerky
Carbohydrate and Protein
1/2 40-30-30 Bar *or* 1 Protein Bar without adding cheese if protein to carbohydrate ratios are adequate.
*Note: See **www.lowcarboptions.com** for protein bar brand recommendations.*

OPTION #5
Protein
3 Cheese Sticks (string cheese) *or* 3 oz. cheese *or* 3 oz. meat *or* 3 oz. turkey or beef jerky *or* 1 scoop Protein Powder
Carbohydrate and Protein
1/4 cup Light Yogurt - any flavor *or* 1/2 cup plain yogurt

OPTION #6 (Fast Food Option)
Breakfast Sandwich: 2 Egg, cheese and meat (w/out top muffin or bun)
Breakfast Burrito: 2 Egg and cheese burritos (tear-off 1/2 tortilla)

OPTION #7
1/3 bagel or 1/2 English muffin or 1 slice toast with 4 oz. cream cheese and/or lox *or* 1 Tbsp. natural peanut or nut butter with 3 cheese sticks *or* 3 oz. cheese *or* 3 oz. meat

OPTION #8
1/3 cup of oatmeal with 2 scoops protein powder *or* omelette

OPTION #9
1 Protein meal replacement shake (add protein powder to milk or water)
*Note: See **www.lowcarboptions.com** for protein powder brand recommendations.*

LUNCH 12:00 NOON AND DINNER 7:00 P.M.
28 GRAMS PROTEIN
10 GRAMS CARBOHYDRATE

OPTION #1
Protein
Chicken (4-6 oz.), Beef (4-6 oz.), Pork (4-6 oz.), Fish (6 oz.) *or* favorite protein choice found on the **Macronutrient Food Unit List**. You may add approximately 1 tablespoon of your favorite sauce (barbecue, teriyaki, etc.) and your favorite spices.
*Note: Vegetarian protein choices are found on the **Macronutrient Food Unit List**.*
Carbohydrate
Favorite Vegetables and/or **Green Salad**- Choose 1 unit (9 carbohydrate grams) of your favorite vegetable choices listed on the **Macronutrient Food Unit List**. You may combine several differentvegetable choices together as long as the total grams of carbohydrate adds up to 1 unit (9 grams). Example: 1 cup of cauliflower and 1/2 cup of broccoli.
Note: See Food Preparation Tips for butter and salad dressing application recommendations.

OPTION #2
Protein
Tuna (6 oz.) or Chicken (4-6 oz.) salad (with mayonnaise) or Deli meat (4-6oz.)
Carbohydrate
1 Tomato or 1 Avocado (medium size) or 1/3 bagel or 1/2 English muffin or 1 low carbohydrate tortilla or 1 slice toast (low carbohydrate brand). You may add mayonnaise and mustard to taste.
*Note: See **www.lowcarboptions.com** for low carbohydrate bread and tortilla brand recommendations.*

OPTION #3 (Fast Food Options)
Garden Fresh Salads: 1 salad with choice of favorite protein (with favorite dressing, no croutons)

Chicken or Steak Burrito: 1 burrito - order extra chicken or steak (no tortilla or tear-off 1/2 of tortilla w/out rice and beans). Guacamole, salsa and sour cream are fine in conservative amounts.
Chicken or Steak Soft Taco: 1 soft taco - order extra chicken or steak (tear-off 1/2 of tortilla). Guacamole, salsa and sour cream are fine in conservative amounts.
Deli-Style or Sub-Sandwich: 1 sandwich with preferred choice of meat or cheese (w/out top bun or protein style-wrapped in lettuce)
Grilled Chicken Sandwich: 1 grilled chicken sandwich (w/out top bun or protein style-wrapped in lettuce)
Rotisserie or Grilled Chicken: 1 skinless thigh, leg, or breast with 1 side cole slaw
Hamburger: Double hamburger or double cheeseburger (w/out top bun or protein style-wrapped in lettuce)
Pizza: 3 slices (eat toppings only - cheese, meat, etc.)
Note: You will maintain a low-fat diet naturally by selecting your protein choices from the Best Choice categories on the Macronutrient Food Unit List.

SNACK 3:30 and (11:00 P.M. - Optional)
7 GRAMS PROTEIN
5 GRAMS CARBOHYDRATE

OPTION #1
1 celery stalk filled with 1 tablespoon of natural peanut or nut butter *or* 2 oz. cream cheese

OPTION #2
1 cheese stick (string cheese) **or 1 oz. cheese** *or* 1 oz. meat with favorite fruit- choose1/2 unit (4.5 carbohydrate grams) of your favorite fruit choice listed on the **Macronutrient Food Unit List.**

OPTION #3
1/4 cup of nuts (any type)

OPTION #4

Hot or Iced cafe latte (1% milk) coffee drink (sugar-free)- Ask the coffee establishment to add a shot of flavored "sugar-free" syrup if available. You may also ask them to blend your iced cafe latte in the blender with the added "sugar-free" syrup for a "sugar-free" ice blended coffee drink. Some coffee establishments have prepared "sugar-free" ice blended coffee drinks.

*Note: See **www.lowcarboptions.com** for sugar-free syrup brand recommendations.*

OPTION #5

1 4-6 oz. glass of milk (skim, 1%, or 2%)

OPTION #6

1/2 cup Light Yogurt - any flavor *or* **1/2 cup of plain yogurt**

OPTION #7

1/2 40-30-30 Bar *or* **Protein Bar**

OPTION #8

1 4-6 oz. glass of wine (dry red or dry white) *or* **light-beer with 1 cheese stick** (string cheese) *or* **1 oz. cheese** *or* **1 oz. meat** *or* **1 oz. turkey or beef jerky**

OPTION #9

1 deviled or hard boiled egg

OPTION #10

1/4 cup ice cream (any brand or flavor) with 1 oz. cheese

NOTE: FREE SNACKS: You may eat certain sugar-free chocolate bars, candies, Jello or pork skins anytime without having to count them as a snack. You may also put a squirt of real whipped cream on the Jello.

Homemade sugar-free popsicles are also an acceptable free snack. Use a popsicle mold and add your favorite sugar-free soda, etc.

*Note: See **www.lowcarboptions.com** for sugar-free chocolate bar and candy brand recommendations.*

Macronutrient Food Units
Protein Choices
Approximately 7 grams Protein Per Unit

Meat and Poultry

Best Choice
Chicken Breast, deli-style, 1.5oz
Chicken Breast, skinless 1.0oz
Turkey Breast, deli-style, 1.5oz
Turkey Breast skinless, 1.0oz
Veal, 1.0oz

Fair Choice
Beef, ground (10% to 15%), 1.5oz
Beef, lean cuts, 1.0oz
Beef, jerky, 1.0oz
Canadian Bacon, lean, 1.0oz
Chicken, dark meat, skinless, 1.0oz
Corned beef, lean, 1.0oz
Duck, 1.5oz
Ham, deli-style, 1.5oz
Ham, lean, 1.0oz
Lamb, lean, 1.0oz
Pork, lean, 1.0oz

Fish and Seafood

Best Choice
Bass, 1.5oz
Blue fish, 1.5oz
Calamari, 1.5oz
Catfish, 1.5oz
Cod, 1.5oz
Clams, 1.5oz
Crabmeat, 1.5oz
Haddock, 1.5oz
Halibut, 1.5oz
Lobster, 1.5oz
 Mackerel, 1.5oz
Salmon, 1.5oz
Sardines, 1.5oz
Scallops, 1.5oz
Shrimp, 1.5oz
Snapper, 1.5oz
Swordfish, 1.5oz
Trout, 1.5oz
Tuna, 1.5oz
Tuna, canned in water,1.0oz

Eggs

Best Choice
Egg whites, 2
Egg substitute, 1/4 cup
Poor Choice
Whole egg, 1

Meat and Poultry (con't)

Fair choice
Pork chop, 1.0oz
Turkey, dark meat, skinless, 1.0oz
Turkey bacon, 3 strips
Turkey sausage, 1.0oz
Turkey burger, 1.0oz
Turkey jerky, 1.0oz
Poor Choice
Bacon, 3 strips
Beef, fatty cuts, 1.0oz
Beef, ground, (more than 15%), 1.5oz
Hot dog (pork or beef), one link
Hot dog (chicken or turkey), one link
Kielbasa, 2.0oz
Liver, beef, 1.0oz
Liver, chicken, 1.0oz
Pepperoni, 1.0oz
Pork sausage, 2 links
Salami, 1.0oz

Protein-Rich Dairy

Best Choice
Cheese, fat free, 1.0oz
Cottage cheese, low fat, 1/4 cup
Cottage cheese, no fat, 1/4 cup
Fair Choice
Cheese, reduced fat, 1.0oz
Mozzarella cheese, skim, 1.0oz
Ricotta cheese, skim, 2,0oz
Cream Cheese, reduced fat, 3.0oz
Poor Choice
Hard Cheeses 1.0oz

**Mixed Protein Carbohydrate
(Contains one unit of protein=7
grams & one unit of
carbohydrate=9 grams)**
Milk, low-fat (1%), 1 cup
Yogurt, plain, 1/2 cup
Nuts, any type, 1oz (approx. 39 pcs)
Peanut butter (natural), 2 Tbsp.
Almond butter (natural), 2 Tbsp.

Vegetarian
Protein powder, 1/3 oz
Soy burger, 1/2 patty
Soy hot dog, 1 link
Soy sausages, 2 links
Tofu, firm or extra firm, 1.0oz
Tofu, soft, 3.0oz

Macronutrient Food Units
Carbohydrate Choices
Approximately 9 grams Carbohydrate Per Unit

Vegetables
Cooked Vegetables
Artichoke, 1 small
Asparagus, 1 cup (12 spears)
Beans, black (canned), 1/3 Cup
Beans, green or wax, 1 Cup
Broccoli, 1 Cup
Brussell Sprouts, 1 Cup
Cabbage, 1 1/2 Cups
Cauliflower, 1 1/2 Cups
Chickpeas, 1 Cup
Collard Greens, 1 Cup
Eggplant, 1 1/2 Cups
Kale, 1 Cup
Kidney Beans (canned), 1 Cup
Leeks, 1/3 Cup
Lentils, 1/3 Cup
Mushrooms (boiled), 1 Cup
Okra (sliced), 1 Cup
Onions (boiled), 1 Cup
Saurekraut, 1 Cup
Swiss chard, 1 Cup
Turnip (mashed), 1 Cup
Turnip greens, 1 1/2 Cups
Yellow Squash, 1 Cup
Zucchini, 1Cup
Raw Vegetables
Avocados (California), 1 medium
Alfalfa sprouts, 1/2 Cup
Bean sprouts, 3 Cups
Broccoli, 2 Cups
Cabbage (shredded), 2 Cups
Cauliflower, 2 Cups
Celery (sliced), 2 Cups or 4 stalks
Cucumber, 1
Cucumber (sliced), 3 Cups
Endive (chopped), 5 Cups
Escarole (chopped), 5 Cups
Green pepper (chopped), 1 1/2 Cups
Green peppers, 2
Hummus, 1/3 Cup
Lettuce, iceberg (1 head)
Lettuce, romaine (chopped), 6 Cup
Mushrooms (chopped), 3 Cups
Onion (chopped), 1 Cup
Radishes (sliced), 2 Cups
Salsa, 1/2 Cup
Snow peas, 1 Cup
Spinach, 4 Cups

Spinach salad, 1
  (2 cups raw spinach, 1/4 cup raw onion, 1/
  2 cup raw mushrooms, and 1/4 cup raw
  tomatoes)
Tomato (chopped), 1 Cup
Tomatoes, 2
Tossed salad, 1
  (2 cups shredded lettuce, 1/4 cup raw green
  pepper, 1/4 cup raw cucumber, and 1/2 cup
  raw tomato)
Water chestnuts, 1/2 Cup

Fruit (fresh, frozen or canned)
Apple, 1/2
Applesauce, 1/3 Cup
Apricots, 3
Blackberries, 1/2 Cup
Blueberries, 1/2 Cup
Cantaloupe, 1/4 melon
Cherries, 7
Fruit cocktail, 1/2 Cup
Grapefruit, 1/2
Grapes, 1/2 Cup
Honeydew melon (cubed), 1/2 Cup
Kiwi, 1
Lemon, 1
Lime, 1
Nectarine, 1/2
Orange, 1/2
Orange mandarin (canned), 1/3 Cup
Peach, 1
Peaches (canned), 1/2 Cup
Pear, 1/3
Pineapple (cubed), 1/2 Cup
Plum, 1
Raspberries, 2/3 Cup
Strawberries, 1 Cup
Tangerine, 1
Watermelon (cubed), 1/2 Cup

Grains and Breads
Oatmeal (slow cooking), 1/3 Cup (cooked) or
1/2oz (dry)
English muffin, 1/2
Bread, 1/2 slice
Hamburger bun, 1/2
Rice, 1/4 Cup
Pasta, 1/4 Cup
Tortilla, corn (6-inch), 1
Tortilla, flour (8-inch), 1/2
Bagel, 1/3

How to Use Your *Total Health* Menu Options

Timing Is Everything

Remember the idea that food is a drug? One key to using drugs effectively is to make sure you take your medicine at regular intervals to maintain an even dosage level. The same principle applies to the *Total Health* eating program.

The key to regulating your blood sugars and burning body fat consistently is to eat every 3 1/2 to 4 hours. This interval promotes optimal metabolism and blood sugar regulation. So I put my patients on a schedule of breakfast at 8 a.m., lunch around noon, a snack around 3:30 in the afternoon, dinner around 7 p.m., and an optional bedtime snack around 11 p.m.

Here's how your daily protein and carbohydrate requirements are portioned out over the course of a day:

If you're at your *ideal body fat and weight*, you can eat a one-to-one ratio of protein to carbohydrates to maintain your weight. For example, if you are in the **Large Body Frame** category, your *daily protein requirement* would be approximately 100 grams of protein to 100 grams of carbohydrate per day.

If you want to put your body into a fat-burning mode of a moderate amount of weight loss of about 2 to 3 pounds a week or about 10 pounds per month, you would limit yourself to 40 grams of carbohydrate per day. Although, you would still eat 100 grams of protein per day.

So for a fat-burning or weight loss mode you would disperse out the 100 grams of protein over the course of the day at the suggested meal times of every 3 1/2 to 4 hours. Therefore, you would have approximately 28 grams of protein at breakfast, lunch and dinner, with about 7 to 10 grams at your two snack times. You would also breakdown the 40 grams of carbohydrates over the course of the day by eating 10 grams of carbohydrates at breakfast, lunch and dinner, with 5 grams at your two snack times.

Note: To avoid losing weight too fast and to reduce potential uncomfortable side-effects and maintaining a healthy rate of weight loss, I start all my patients at 40 grams of carbohydrates per day.

If you follow your customized *Total Health* Protein-Rich, Favorable-Carbohydrate Prepared Meal Menu Options, you can expect to lose 2 to 4 pounds of excess weight the first week or 8 to 10 pounds per month. If you have less weight to lose or a smaller body frame you can expect to lose 1 to 2 pounds of excess weight or 6 to 8 pounds per month.

If you experience a prolonged period of little or no weight loss, your customized menu should be adjusted to "jump start" your progress. If you experience such a plateau, simply cut your carbohydrate consumption at each meal in half. If this doesn't work, you may want to consider the *20 Tips for Breaking a Weight Loss Plateau* in the following section of **Total Health Success Tips**.

Creating your Own Customized Meal Menu Options

Creating your own menu options is easy. Just use your protein and carbohydrate food unit lists and the protein and carbohydrate allotment for each meal. The amount can be found on your *Total Health* menu according to your *body frame size* under "Breakfast", "Lunch", and "Dinner."

Let's take breakfast for a **Small Body Frame** for example.

Breakfast
21 grams of protein
10 grams of carbohydrates

On your protein food unit list, you'll notice that 7 grams of protein equals one unit. In this example, you're allowed 21 grams of protein. Let's say you want cottage cheese as your protein choice. How much can you have? If 1/4 cup equals 7 grams of protein, you can have three units, or 3/4 cup of cottage cheese.

On your carbohydrate food unit list, you'll notice that 9 grams of carbohydrates equals one unit. In this example, you're allowed 10 grams of carbohydrates. Let's say you want pineapple as your carbohydrate choice. How much can you have. If a 1/2 cup of pineapple equals 9 grams of carbohydrate, you can have one unit, or a 1/2 cup of pineapple.

You can create the same formula to create your own lunch, dinner and snack options. Simply choose your favorite protein entrée and carbohydrate choices as long as you stay within the 21 grams of protein and 10 grams of carbohydrates or less at each meal.

Note: Your Total Health program offers an infinite variety of protein and carbohydrate combinations. Check out the recipes in the Total Health recipe section of this book or over 120 recipes at www.totalhealthdoc.com and see for yourself. However, during your first couple weeks on the program, for your convenience, we recommend that you follow the options on your Total Health menu.

What To Expect

• The First Week

During your first week of living in *Total Health*, you may feel an initial dip in energy levels and hunger pangs. This is a natural adjustment reaction. Your body is learning to do without the cheap sugar rush to which it's grown accustomed. Instead of burning carbohydrates for energy, your body's metabolism is starting to burn the stored sugars in your liver and fat reserves.

You may experience light-headedness and/or a low-grade headache, which are typical symptoms of sugar withdrawals. After 2 to 3 days, these symptoms will pass.

More frequent urination is also natural. Your kidneys probably aren't used to processing up to 8 glasses of water daily. Adequate water intake is important to prevent constipation and to help the kidneys eliminate natural by-products of the fat breakdown process through urine.

Depending on how much weight you have to lose and your daily carbohydrate allotment, you may lose between 2 and 5 pounds the first week. If you do not experience weight loss the first week, don't be alarmed. Your metabolic hormones may need more time to adjust.

Many people report a substantial increase in energy and mental sharpness by the end of the first week.

Note: Many times, women will not experience weight loss before and during the menstrual cycle. This is natural and due to increased fluid retention.

• The Second Week

By the second week, any headaches or feelings of lightheadedness should be replaced by a marked increase in energy. Any hunger pangs should also be gone.

When You Reach Your Weight Goal

Once you've reached your *ideal body fat and weight,* you can simply increase your carbohydrate intake to a one-to-one ratio of protein to carbohydrates to maintain your weight.

At this point you may also introduce some of the more "unfavorable" or "high-glycemic" types of carbohydrates back into your meal plan. This would be carbohydrate choices such as rice, pasta, potatoes, etc.

Here's an example of what we're saying:

Let's say you're a Large Body Frame size and are allowed 28 grams of protein at each meal and 10 grams of carbohydrates in the form of fiber-rich fruits and vegetables during the weight loss phase.

Now that you're at your target weight and are allowed a one-to-one ratio of protein to carbohydrates, you would be able to have approximately 28 grams of protein to 27 grams of carbohydrates.

You could now consider allowing yourself to have a few of the "unfavorable" carbohydrate choice as part of your total carbohydrate allotment as outlined in the following example.

Protein (28 Grams)

Chicken (4-6 oz.), Beef (4-6 oz.), Pork (4-6 oz.), Fish (6 oz.) *or* **favorite protein choice.**

Carbohydrates (27 Grams)

Favorite Vegetables and/or **Green Salad**- Choose 3 units (27 carbohydrate grams) of your favorite vegetable choices. You may combine several different carbohydrate choices together as long as the total grams of carbohydrate adds up to 3 units (27 grams). Example: 1/4 cup of pasta or rice w/ 1 cup of broccoli.

Caution: Don't fall back into the trap of eating too many "unfavorable" high-glycemic carbohydrates. We still want you choosing the "favorable" low-glycemic carbohydrates in the form of fiber-rich fruits and vegetables the majority of the time!

Total Health Success Tips

Weigh Yourself Once a Week. This is necessary to monitor your progress on your *Total Health* program. Some people choose to weigh themselves daily. Also there may be times when your body is re-distributing muscle and fat percentages. This means that you may gain 2 pounds of muscle (which is good) and lose 2 pounds of fat. The scale weight won't reflect weight loss, but your body fat percentage went down due to the 2 pounds of fat loss. This translates into inches lost!

In fact, stepping on a scale daily may prove unnecessarily discouraging. That's because it's rare to see noticeable weight loss from day-to-day. Many times, weight loss occurs on the last few days of the week. So do yourself a favor: Focus on following your *Total Health* plan, instead of obsessing daily about the number on your scale. The program works! The pounds will come off! If the weight still isn't coming off after a week or more, we suggest the following tips for breaking a true weight loss plateau:

20 Tips for Breaking a Weight Loss Plateau

1. *Don't Give Up* - Your continued search will probably find the problem and correct it.
2. *Check for Hidden Sources of Sugar* - Sugar goes under many different names & in many cases does NOT appear on the label. Many vitamin tablets have sugar fillers. CHECK!
3. *Perhaps You're Cheating* - If you think it's too small to matter, better check again. (Chewing gum, etc.)
4. *You May Be Keeping Your Food Intake Too Low* - Many times you carry over habits from other diets & eat too little. Remember to eat the full amount of protein at each scheduled meal and snack time.

5. *Are You Eating Your Three Meals and Two snacks per Day?* - A frequent eating schedule will provide a constant source of energy without the insulin rebound. Remember to eat every 3 1/2 to 4 hours and don't skip meals or snacks! Your body goes into a conservation mode and you will quit losing weight when you don't eat.

6. *You May Not Have reduced Your Carbohydrate Intake Enough* - You may need to reduce your carbohydrate intake even further in the beginning if your body is resistant to weight loss.

7. *Check Your Mineral Balance* - You may have a mineral imbalance. Such as zinc/copper or other essential trace minerals.

8. *You May Be Losing Too Much Potassium* - Salt or potassium shortages are common in the first stages of low carbohydrate diets. You may need to increase your salt intake or take potassium supplements.

9. *Try Increasing Your Levels of Exercise* - Exercise can improve circulation, stabilize blood sugars & other important metabolic benefits.

10. *Check Your Vitamins* - Certain vitamin mixtures may contain hidden carbohydrates. Colloidal or liquid mineral mixtures are many times in a juice formula containing hidden sugars, etc. Be sure to check the carbohydrate amounts on the label.

11. *Food Additives* - Over a billion pounds of chemicals are added to our food every year. You may be allergic to some of them. Check for dyes in soft drinks, fillers,etc.

12. *Too Much Coffee or Tea* - Even though I allow the consumption of coffee and tea, too much can stimulate the release of insulin. This may result in a temporary lift in energy followed by hunger, fatigue and slower weight loss.

13. *Smoking* - Some people will not respond to the diet unless smoking is stopped. Smoking uses up vitamin C & stimulates the adrenal gland.

14. *Excessive Alcohol Consumption* - Even though I recommend distilled spirits or hard alcohol are over beer and wine

because of zero carbohydrate content. Excessive alcohol consumption stimulates an insulin response.

15. *Medications* - Many drugs, even aspirin, can cause hypoglycemia. Watch out for hormones, amphetamines, diuretics, antihistamines, anti-inflammatory drugs, analgesics, anticoagulants, anti-hypoglycemics, antibiotics, tranquilizers, clofibrate, acetaminophen, and propanolol.

16. *Prior Use of Diet Pills* - Sometimes it isn't what you are taking, but what you were taking that slows down your weight loss progress.

17. *Hormone Replacement Therapy* - Will slow down weight loss and stimulate the production of insulin. Estrogen (used in birth control pills) and testosterone have much the same effect.

18. *Too Much Salt Can Lead to Fluid Retention* - After 2 to 3 weeks on the diet, the body partially adapts and excessive salt can cause some fluid retention.

19. *Portion Control* - You may be eating too much protein at each meal. Remember to stick to your *Daily Protein Requirement*. Even though carbohydrates count more, caloric intake is still a factor during the weight loss phase.

20. *Thyroid Problems* - Your problem may be a low thyroid. If you suffer from low body temperature, cold hands and feet, dry skin, brittle hair and nails, you may have hypothyroidism. Consult with your physician for a blood test to rule out the possibility of a thyroid problem.

Additional *Total Health* Success Tips:

Choose healthy carbohydrates in the form of fiber-rich fruits and vegetables with a low glycemic index. These are listed on the *Macronutrient Food Unit List*. Strictly limit pasta, rice, bread and grains.

Choose sources of healthy fats such as olive oil and nut oils. You will maintain a low-fat diet naturally by eating lean meat, poultry, seafood, low-fat dairy and vegetarian protein.

Drink plenty of water, up to 8 glasses a day. You may also choose any sugar free beverage such as diet sodas, Crystal Light, etc. Hot tea, iced tea and coffee are allowed. Use sugar substitutes to sweeten. If using artificial sweeteners such as Aspartame is unappealing, try Splenda® which is made from sucralose. Stevia - a natural sweetener is also available at health stores. See the **Sugar Alternatives** section in this chapter for more details on sugar substitutes.

We also suggest the use of sugar-free syrups for coffee, plain yogurts, etc. There are many great tasting sugar-free flavors such as chocolate, hazelnut, caramel, vanilla, etc. See our recommendations for the best manufacturers of low carbohydrate products at **www.lowcarboptions.com**.

A glass of wine or lite beer is allowed but not by themselves. Because these beverages contain up to 4 grams of carbohydrates, you must consume them with some protein. Have your wine or beer with lunch or dinner or with some cheese as a snack. Mixed drinks are also acceptable as long as you use a sugar free mixer. Example: Vodka with sugar-free tonic.

Believe it or not, distilled alcohols such as vodka, rum, whiskey, gin, etc., have zero net carbohydrate value. Therefore, distilled alcohols are the preferred alcoholic beverages of choice.

Get your fiber. Adequate fiber intake is essential for healthy digestion. To make sure you get enough fiber, use over-the-counter supplements or sugar-free orange flavored Metamucil mixed into 8-10 ounces of drinking water. Drink up to 2 glasses a day. Go to www.lowcarboptions.com for a complete listing of recommended fiber supplements.

Take a high quality vitamin and mineral supplement daily. If you're confused about what kind of supplement to purchase you may want to visit www.lowcarboptions.com for our top recommendations for nutritional supplements.

Use the "ballpark" technique. When dining out or when in doubt, this is an easy way to make sure you eat the proper amount of protein and carbohydrates. Keep your protein choice (meat, poultry or fish) to a portion about the size of the palm of your hand - roughly 4 ounces. Choose a salad or vegetable portion about twice the size of your protein portion. Example: Caesar salad with grilled chicken. (Remember to take it easy on the croutons and don't eat any bread).

Food Preparation Tips

Hot or Iced Cafe Latte: Keep your drink sugar-free. If available, you may sweeten your latte with a shot of "sugar-free" syrup.

Meat, Poultry and Fish: Cook meat by grilling, broiling, baking or stir-frying.

Salad Dressing: Use olive oil and vinegar. Olive oil is an excellent source of linoleic acid - an essential fatty acid. You may also use regular dressings such as Ranch dressing, etc., but check the carbohydrate content on the label. Stay away from low-fat and no-fat dressings, they're loaded with sugar.

Vegetables: You may melt a pad of real butter over your veggies. Do not use margarine because margarine contains partially hydrogenated vegetable oil, a high source of unfavorable trans fatty acids.

Yogurt: Use yogurt sweetened with sugar substitutes. If you don't like artificial sweeteners, flavor a 1/2 cup of plain yogurt with vanilla extract and natural sweetener Stevia or Splenda(r) or your favorite sugar-free syrup flavor to taste.

Sugar Alternatives

Artificial sweeteners or sugar substitutes have been on the market for several years and have opened a whole new world for people from low carb followers to diabetics who want to enjoy sweets without adversely affecting blood sugars.

The use of various non-nutritive and nutritive sweeteners is acceptable in the management of diabetes and supported by most health professionals. Regardless of their popularity and availability, dietitians agree that these products can be a part of a healthy diet but they are not the answer to freely consuming desserts, candies and beverages.

One of the first questions most people ask is, "Are these sweeteners safe to consume?"

In order for sweeteners to be offered on the supermarket shelves, they have to be approved by the FDA. This means they are proven safe for human consumption. For most sweeteners, the government has set an acceptable daily intake (ADI), a value based on medical research. This is the average amount of sweetener a person could eat or drink every day of their lives without causing harm.

The ADI is based on a persons' body weight and covers a wide safety margin. It is much easier for children to go over the safe amount, compared to adults, because their weight is usually less than adults. Women who are pregnant or breastfeeding should talk to their physician regarding the use of sweeteners.

However, some people are still not comfortable using artificial sweeteners, and prefer to incorporate "real sugar" into their meal plan. This will inhibit the success of weight loss due to the high carbohydrate content.

Sweeteners are separated into two categories , **nutritive** (containing calories) and **non-nutritive** (containing no calories). Nutritive sweeteners are broken down by the body and therefore provide energy, but do not contribute any other essential nutrients. *Non-nutritive sweeteners* do not provide any energy to the diet.

Nutritive Sweeteners

SUCROSE

The term "sugar" is used to refer to monosaccharides and disaccharides collectively, while specific sugars are referred to by their proper names; sucrose, fructose, lactose, glucose and so on. Although the consumer is confronted by a wide variety of sugars; sucrose, raw sugar, turbinado sugar, brown sugar, honey, corn syrups, there is no significant difference in the nutritional content or the calories each provides and therefore, no advantage of one over another.

Sucrose is the most commonly used sugar. Although it is evident that human beings have an innate desire for sweetness as previously discussed, there is no suggestion that sweet foods are essential to health.

FRUCTOSE

Fructose syrups have been promoted as sweeteners for people with diabetes, but will still cause a rise in blood sugars. Fructose is a naturally occurring monosaccharide. It offers fewer calories compared to other starches and sugar as it provides the same amount of energy, 4 kcal/gram. Fructose is most effective as a sweetening agent in high acid and cold foods, such as citrus drinks.

Small amounts of fructose impart a sweeter taste in food products than the usual amount of sucrose because fructose is approximately 1 to 1.8 times as sweet as sucrose. Because of the cost of pure crystalline fructose, high-fructose corn syrups containing 42%, 55%, or 90% fructose are generally used by food manufacturers. The remaining carbohydrate in those syrups is mainly glucose.

Fructose travels mainly to the liver and can be used there without the need for insulin. In the absence of insulin, fructose can be converted to glucose in the liver and therefore can contribute to an increase in blood glucose rather than being stored as glycogen.

Unlike sucrose and glucose, which cause quick changes to the blood glucose levels and can disrupt the metabolic control of a person with diabetes, fructose is absorbed more slowly and causes fewer changes in blood glucose levels.

Fructose-sweetened products can still make a significant contribution to caloric intake and therefore can't be considered as a freely-used sugar alternative.

SUCRALOSE (SPLENDA®)

Sucralose is the common name for the only calorie-free sweetener created from ordinary sugar. It looks and tastes like sugar, but isn't broken down in the body and hence provides no calories. On average, sucralose is about 600 times sweeter than sugar.

Sucralose can be used like sugar in a wide range of foods and beverages due to its sweetness intensity, good water solubility and excellent product stability. Sucralose can be found in baked goods, drinks, frozen desserts, chewing gum, milk products, salad dressings, tabletop sweeteners, and alcoholic beverages.

Sucralose does not build up in the body nor does it promote cavities. Many studies have been done and evaluated on animals and humans over the past two decades and sucralose has been approved for use in Canada since 1991.

The ADI of sucralose is 15 mg/kg. SPLENDA is available in two "tabletop" forms: granular and packet. The granular measures, pours and can be used like sugar even in cooking and baking, cup-for-cup. The granular form has 2 calories per teaspoon which are attributable to the carrier, maltodextrin.

The packets can be used to sweeten coffee, tea and other beverages and to sprinkle on fruit, cereal and desserts. Each packet contains the equivalent of 2 teaspoons of sugar.

SORBITOL, MANNITOL, AND XYLITOL

Sorbitol, mannitol and xylitol are the most common *sugar alcohols.*

Sorbitol and mannitol are naturally found in small amounts in some fruits and vegetables and are often used as sweeteners in many products. They are both half as sweet as sucrose, therefore, more must be used to reach the same level of sweetness.

Sorbitol provides about 4 kcal/gram. Sorbitol and other sugar alcohols are more slowly absorbed than other carbohydrates such as sucrose and glucose, requiring from 1 to 8 hours for complete absorption. Due to this reduced rate of absorption, caloric content may be slightly less depending on the amount used in the product.

Sorbitol is rapidly converted to fructose in the liver. Initially, it's not directly dependent on insulin; however, sorbitol's absorption later follows the same breakdown as fructose. The sugar alcohols are relatively free of carcinogens (cancer causing chemicals) because they're fermented more slowly by bacteria in the mouth than are other sugars.

Depending upon the gastrointestinal sensitivity of the individual and the person's body weight, abdominal gas, discomfort and diarrhea can occur after consuming significant amounts of sugar alcohol. Mannitol can cause some diarrhea and abdominal complaints if more than 20 grams are consumed daily, for sorbitol it's over 50 grams per day , however, some people's tolerance levels are as low as 10 grams per day.

Therefore, it's recommended that foods containing sorbitol be limited to portions containing 20 kcal or less. Products that contain small amounts of sorbitol are hard candy, sugarless gum, jams, jellies and "dietetic" or "diabetic" chocolates.

ASPARTAME (EQUAL®, NUTRASWEET®)

Aspartame, is used as a sweetening ingredient in a variety of foods and beverages. Equal® is a low-calorie tabletop sweetener and is available in packets and tablets.

Aspartame, a white odorless crystalline powder, is considered a nutritive sweetener since its major constituents are two naturally occurring amino acids, aspartic acid and phenylalanine. Aspartame is broken down by the body the same way as other proteins in our foods.

Aspartame is 180-200 times sweeter than sucrose, therefore a much smaller amount is needed to achieve a sweet taste thus providing less energy than sucrose. However, because of the minimal number of calories provided by aspartame, it could also be grouped with the non-nutritive sweeteners.

Unlike sucrose, aspartame's commercial use is limited as it does break down and loses its sweetness when used in baking at high temperatures or when combined with acidic foods. Therefore, the Food Regulations allow aspartame as a sweetener and flavor enhancer only in certain foods.

The question of the stability of aspartame in liquid under storage conditions has also been raised. The FDA has determined that although this might result in a marginally acceptable product from a taste standpoint, it would not lead to an unsafe product.

Aspartame is not known to result in any harmful effects for most people. However, there are individuals who suffer from a hereditary disease known as phenylketonuria and who must control their intake of phenylalanine, one of the amino acids in aspartame. Labels contain the information of foods containing aspartame, declaring the total of calories, protein, carbohydrate and aspartame and fat per 100 ml or 100g.

There have been many public safety concerns about aspartame, as well as some reported reactions to the product. Confirmation of reactions to food ingredients and food additives is always difficult, especially when not diagnosed by physicians specializing in food allergies. The FDA is closely monitoring such complaints. Current labeling requirements for food additives is improving to enable those who wish to avoid any specific substances to do so.

There are some people who may claim to be particularly sensitive to the ingestion of aspartame and experience a wide variety of mild nonspecific symptoms. Headaches, irritability, failure to lose weight or to control blood sugars have all been reported.

Research has not been able to confirm aspartame sensitivity or describe how symptoms could be triggered metabolically. *However, it seems sensible to limit aspartame intake in people who experience these sensitivities.*

STEVIA (STEE -vee-uh)

Stevia is a type of South American shrub. The leaves have been used for centuries by native peoples in Paraguay and Brazil to sweeten their beverages. Stevioside, the main ingredient in stevia (the two terms are often used interchangeable), is virtually calorie-free and hundreds of times sweeter than table sugar.

You can buy stevia leaves or powder in most health food stores, but the herb has not been approved as a food additive for sweetening foods as there is not enough evidence to determine if it's safe or to estimate what levels of stevia are safe to consume.

Last year, the scientific panel that reviews the safety of food ingredients for the European Union concluded that the main ingredient in stevia, stevioside isn't acceptable as a sweetener because of unresolved concerns about its toxicity. The main issues are the possible reproductive problems in males, and the possible risk of cancer from the conversion of stevioside to steviol which may promote cancer.

Also, very large amounts of stevioside can interfere with the absorption of carbohydrates in animals and disrupt the conversion of food into energy within the cells.

We still don't know enough about stevia and that's why the government needs to insist on companies to do more and better testing.

Non-Nutritive Sweeteners

ACESULFAME POTASSIUM (K)

Acesulfame K (ace-K) is a white crystalline, calorie free sweetening ingredient. It's almost 200 times sweeter than sucrose and is commercially sold under the brand name Sunett. It is used in thousands of products, offering low-calorie, low-sugar food choices to incorporate into a healthy diet. It gives a sweet taste with no lingering aftertaste. Ace-K is calorie free, sodium free and does not promote tooth decay.

It's heat stable, therefore, you can cook and bake with ace-K. In Canada, ace- K has received Health Protection Branch Approval (HPB) for use in tabletop sweeteners, beverages, desserts, chewing gums, baked goods, confections, breath fresheners, fruit spreads, and salad dressings.

Ace-K can be blended with nutritive sweeteners. The blending of nutritive and non-nutritive sweeteners produces the desired level of sweetness in the product while needing substantially less of the individual sweeteners. More and more food companies are using sweetener combinations because blending provides advantages for both the food manufacturer and the consumer. The food company is able to use less total sweetener while providing the consumer with an improved taste profile in the end product.

Ace-K requires no health warning/information statement, however, it may be blended with one that does require a statement. Ace-K can be blended with nutritive sweeteners such as fructose, sorbitol and mannitol. It has been concluded that ace-K does not promote tooth decay.

Studies with animals with chemically-induced diabetes have shown that ace-K has no effect on glucose, cholesterol, total glycerol in the blood serum nor is it cancer-causing. Ace-K was fed in progressively larger doses in excess of the possible consumption by individuals. Pregnant women may incorporate products containing ace- K into their balanced diet.

The chemical structure of ace-K contains the sulfur atom, however, there is no concern that people who are allergic to sulfa drugs or products containing sulfites will have a reaction because ace-K's properties are different from products containing sulfites and sulfa drugs.

Potassium makes up about 20% by weight of the total amount of ace-K added to a product. This amount of potassium contributed by ace-K is minimal compared to the average daily intake of potassium from other food sources. For example, only 10 mg of potassium is contributed by ace-K in the sweetening equivalent of 2 tsp of sucrose, while a medium sized banana contains 440 mg of potassium, an orange 263 mg, sweet potato 394 mg.

The average daily intake (ADI) of ace-K is 15 mg/kg. For a 60 kg (132 lbs) person, this corresponds to 900 mg everyday for a person's lifetime or about 200 gm or almost 1/2 lb of sucrose equivalent.

Ace-K is not broken down nor does it in the human body, therefore it has no caloric value. It's rapidly absorbed after ingestion, and is then rapidly eliminated, unchanged in the urine. Over 98% of ace-K is excreted within 24 hours in humans.

SACCAHRIN (Hermesetas®, Sweet 'N Low®)

Almost immediately after it was discovered as the first man-made sugar substitute, saccharin has been the sweetener of controversy. Saccharin is 300 to 400 times sweeter than sucrose and was used extensively in many foods. In 1977, saccharin was banned because it was found to cause urinary bladder cancer in animals.

To date, scientific studies have found no conclusive link between saccharin and bladder cancer, although the need for more research is indicated. Saccharin was made available as a table-top sweetener provided it was only sold in pharmacies. It was labeled to indicate pregnant women must discuss the use of saccharin with their physician before consuming.

Cyclamates (Hermesetas®, Finesweet®, Sucaryl®, SugarTwin®

The salts of cyclamic acid, are about 30 to 50 times as sweet as sucrose. Similar to saccharin, cyclamates have been banned in the United States since 1970 on the results of animal studies related to bladder cancer. Even though the Food and Drug Administration review of the safety studies concluded that evidence doesn't indicate that cyclamates by themselves cause cancer, it recommended that additional studies be done to address specific issues.

SUMMARY

The major benefit from use of sweeteners is a perceived improvement in the variety of food choices, particularly for people with diabetes. The possible risk from any one sweetener can be minimized by moderate use of a variety of sweeteners so that the individual ingests less of any specific sweetener. Sweeteners should be used within the context of an otherwise nutritious and well-balanced diet.

Current evidence indicates that use of sweeteners available to consumers at reasonable levels of intake are safe and are not associated with any serious risks for disease or to the health of well persons. It's important that the public have a choice of various non-nutritive sweeteners, with safe and reasonable guidelines on how to use each type.

As new sweeteners become available, they must receive the same rigorous testing to which previously approved sweeteners have been subjected. Research into the possible risks of long-term uses of non-nutritive sweeteners, either alone or in combination, should continue.

Reading Food Labels for Net Effective Carbohydrate Count

As you may be aware, there is considerable concern and confusion in regard to the nutritional labeling of food products in the low carbohydrate food industry.

The confusion lies in the way carbohydrates are viewed and calculated. Food is divided into five main categories:

* Fat
* Protein
* Moisture
* Ash (minerals)
* Carbohydrates

The government calculates by *difference*, which means anything that is not Fat, Protein, Moisture, or Ash is lumped into the carbohydrate category. This includes sugars and sugar alcohols. Carbohydrates can be further subdivided:

* Sugars (sucrose, lactose, maltose, fructose, glucose)
* Fibers
* Sugar alcohols (maltitol, sorbitol, lactitiol, isomalt)

Low carbohydrate food providers recognize the government's method of categorizing ingredients as carbohydrates, but we must take into account the effects of the various ingredients on the body.

They have designed a new label to meet the government's methods and requirements. Where they used to omit the sugar alcohols from the total carb count on the nutritional panel, they now include it. In addition to this change, they now include a Carbohydrate Facts Panel (see below) to show you the net effective carbs. These net effective carbs include only those carbs that cause a noted effect on your blood sugar levels.

Fiber and sugar alcohols can be subtracted from the total carbohydrate count.

Example:

Total Carbs	32g
- Fiber	-10g
- Sugar alcohols	-20g
Net Effective Carbs	**2g**

Protein and Carbohydrate Combinations:

Meat or Chicken Stir-Fry with vegetables is a tasty way to combine protein and carbohydrates in an easy one dish meal. Flavor with teriyaki or your favorite sauce.

Chicken or Steak Fajitas are another good option. Add guacamole and sour cream as long as you count the guacamole as part of your carbohydrate allotment. Stay away from the chips and tortillas.

Chicken Ceasar Salad, Chinese Chicken Salad or Cobb Salad are three other good combination choices, especially when dining out. Just be sure to ask for your salad dressing on the side and don't over do it.

Oriental Cuisine Tips: Protein/carb combinations such as beef and broccoli, almond chicken, or shrimp and vegetables are good choices. Egg drop or hot and sour soup are okay. Remember, use the ballpark technique to watch your portions and stay away from rice, noodles, and fortune cookies!

Japanese Cuisine: Choose sashimi, chicken or steak teriyaki instead of sushi, which contains rice. Your may also have miso soup and cucumber or lettuce salad with your protein entree.

Micronutrients (Vitamins and Minerals)

If you're like most Americans, chances are you've got at least one - and probably several - half-full bottles of vitamin and mineral supplements in your medicine cabinet.

And no wonder. It seems every day some new study or article or health guru says Vitamin X or Mineral Y helps you stay healthy or prevent some horrible disease. Then every other day, a new study or article or guru says the stuff you just bought is no good. Worse, Vitamin X can actually cause a different, but equally horrible disease. Besides, what you really need is Vitamin Z!

Thanks to an increasingly health conscious public and relentless marketing, sales of vitamins and other nutritional supplements have skyrocketed! According to the Council for Responsible Nutrition, a trade group for the supplement industry, an estimated 100 million Americans are spending $6.5 billion a year on vitamins, minerals and nutritional supplements. That's up from $3 billion in 1990.

Two factors are driving the explosive growth in supplement sales. First, as Baby Boomers get older, more and more people are becoming active participants in their own health care. This consumer health care movement is being fueled by easier access to medical information and acceptance of health care options such as acupuncture and chiropractic by traditional medical organizations.

The other reason for all the marketing hype about nutritional supplements is the Dietary Supplement Health and Education Act of 1994. This law allows supplement makers to market their products as "dietary supplements" and thus avoid the scientific scrutiny and expense of the FDA prescription drug review process. As long as supplement manufacturers do not claim their products offer specific health benefits, they're free to sell their wares over the counter, through mail order and over the Internet.

Confused?

The following pages will help you sort through the hype. We'll start with a brief review of vitamin and mineral fundamentals. Then we'll take a closer look at how vitamin and mineral supplements, water and fiber contribute to optimal health.

Vitamin and Mineral Basics

Even though we can increase our energy levels, reduce body fat, and increase our immunity against sickness through the *Total Health* eating plan, the complete system requires the micronutrients (vitamins and minerals) for ultimate performance.

Micronutrients - commonly known as vitamins and minerals - are essential for life. They perform a multitude of functions which involve the efficient use and disposal of the *macronutrients* (protein, carbohydrates and fat). The body isn't able to produce micronutrients and we're unable to get enough even with a proper diet.

This is largely due to increased environmental factors such as air pollution and decreased food nutrient value due to the depleted mineral values in our soil. Therefore, we must choose the appropriate multivitamin/mineral supplement that will ensure we have the necessary amounts of these essential micronutrients for our body to mange the complex functions required for an active healthy lifestyle.

Before we can choose the *right vitamin and mineral supplement*, we must first learn about the terms and definitions associated with vitamins and minerals.

Vitamins are organic and allow your body to process carbohydrates, proteins and fats. They also act as catalysts by triggering or speeding up chemical reactions. There are a total of

13 vitamins, which nutritionists classify into two groups, *Fat-Soluble and Water-Soluble.*

The "fat-soluble" vitamins are - A, D, E and K - They're called "fat-soluble" because they're stored in your body's fat. They're usually found together in the fats and oils of food and require bile for absorption.

Once absorbed, they're stored in the liver and fatty tissues until the body needs them. Deficiencies of the *fat soluble* vitamins are likely when the diet is consistently low in them or when they're lost in undigested fat.

Any disease that prevents fat absorption, such as liver disease that prevents bile production, can bring about deficiencies of the *fat soluble* vitamins. Deficiencies are also likely when people eat diets that are extremely low in fat.

Vitamins A and D can act somewhat like hormones, directing cells to store, and release or convert substances. Vitamin E circulates all over the body preventing oxidative damage to tissues.

The other nine are "water-soluble" and aren't stored in large amounts in your body. The water-soluble vitamins include vitamin C and the eight B vitamins - thiamine (B-1), riboflavin (B-2), niacin (B-3), pyridoxine (B-6), pantothenic acid, cyanocobalamin (B-12), biotin and folic acid (folate).

The body absorbs them easily and just as easily excretes them in the urine. The *water-soluble* vitamins help the body metabolize carbohydrates, lipids, and amino acids. The "B" vitamins are considered co-enzymes, which are small molecules that combine with enzymes to make them active. The "B" vitamins work together with enzymes in the metabolism of energy, nutrients, and making of new cells.

Minerals are inorganic substances that promote a variety of important biochemical processes. There are 15 dietary minerals, which nutritionists also classify into two groups: *Major minerals* are needed in amounts greater than 100 milligrams a day. *Trace minerals* are needed in amounts less than 100 milligrams a day.

The *major minerals* include calcium, phosphorus, magnesium, sodium, chloride, potassium and sulfur. The trace minerals include iron, iodine, copper, chromium, fluoride, manganese, molybdenum, selenium and zinc.

The *trace minerals* required for human health are iron, iodine, copper, manganese, zinc, boron, selenium, and chromium. These are used by the body to burn fat, build muscle and strengthen bones as well as promoting healing and oxygen delivery to the cells.

How Much Do You Need?

When it comes to taking vitamins and mineral supplements, the question of "how much?" is a source of continuing controversy.

Most established medical, scientific and nutritional sources say you get all the vitamins and minerals you need from eating a balanced diet. Follow the general nutritional guidelines such as the Recommended Dietary Allowances (RDAs) and you'll be fine.

The Balanced Diet Problem

Do you eat a balanced diet? Do you know anyone who does? That's the big problem with the notion that the food you eat provides all the vitamins and minerals you need. Most Americans don't eat the wide variety of food necessary to obtain the right amount of the micronutrients they need.

For example, in a study published in the *New England Journal of Medicine* in March 1998, researchers from the Harvard Medical School estimated that 40 percent of Americans may have Vitamin D deficiencies. Forty percent!

Our rushed, junk food, no-time-for-breakfast or lunch, prepackaged, processed, frozen-food culture does not encourage a balanced diet. And as you know, if you're not eating the right balance of foods in the right amount, vitamin and mineral deficiencies may be the least of your problems! No multivitamin supplement will compensate for lousy eating habits.

Are the RDAs Enough?

Since 1941, the Food and Nutrition Board of the Institute of Medicine, National Academy of Sciences, has set RDAs to recommend the minimum amount of vitamins and minerals needed to prevent diseases caused by vitamin and mineral deficiencies.

For years, this approach has been criticized by a growing

andincreasingly vocal number of respected medical researchers and doctors. They argue that the intake levels dictated by the RDAs are just enough to help you survive, not thrive. Instead, vitamins and minerals should be taken in amounts that prevent chronic diseases and promote optimal health, a state in which your body functions at its best.

It's taken some time, but the government nutrition experts, the folks who set the official nutritional standards, are catching up. Slowly but surely RDAs are being reset to recommend higher amounts of specific vitamins and minerals.

In 1997, the Board announced that the RDAs were now just one part of an expanded set of nutritional guidelines called Dietary Reference Intakes (DRIs). The DRIs reflect the latest scientific consensus on the role vitamins and minerals play in optimum health. For example, the first DRI report, on calcium, revised intake levels upwards to prevent bone loss caused by osteoporosis instead of just preventing a calcium deficiency.

New DRIs on folate and other B vitamins were published in 1998. As funding becomes available, new DRIs - which will include updated and expanded RDAs - will be set for other nutrient groups, including antioxidants, macronutrients, trace minerals, and fiber.

As nutritional research becomes more influential in mainstream medicine, it's now routine for M.D.s to prescribe high doses of vitamins and minerals to address specific conditions or diseases. For example, high doses of calcium are often prescribed for women to prevent osteoporosis. High doses of folic acid are often prescribed for women as part of good pre- and post-natal care. People who suffer from anemia usually need iron supplements.

The *Total Health* Approach to Vitamins and Minerals

1. **Eat a protein-rich, favorable-carbohydrate diet.** The best way to make sure your body is supplied with a continuing source of essential micronutrients is to eat a wide variety of foods. It bears repeating that no vitamin or mineral supplement can compensate for the benefits of eating a properly balanced protein-rich, favorable-carbohydrate

diet. That's why they're called vitamin and mineral supplements - not replacements.

2. **Do no harm!** Do not take megadoses of vitamins or minerals unless prescribed by your doctor to treat a specific deficiency. Some vitamin advocates go so far as to recommend massive doses of certain vitamins to ward off ailments ranging from cancer to impotence. The FDA and mainstream medicine regard these perpetual vitamin fads as quackery - and often dangerous. For example, large amounts of vitamin A can contribute to liver damage. Excess doses of vitamin D can contribute to kidney damage. Iron, zinc, chromium and selenium can be toxic at just five times the RDA. The most common cause of poisoning deaths among children is adult-strength iron supplements.

3. **Use vitamin and mineral supplements as nutritional insurance.** The *Total Health* program provides your body with the essential micronutrients it needs from two sources: the food you eat and a high-quality vitamin and mineral supplement.

How to Choose the Right Vitamin and Mineral Supplement

The following ingredients are essential when choosing a high-quality vitamin and mineral supplement. If you are confused about what kind of supplement to purchase or have any questions about particular ingredients, etc., you may visit **www.lowcarboptions.com**.

Antioxidants

Antioxidants counter the harmful effects of a chemical chain reaction caused by free radicals. Free radicals are chemically reactive oxygen molecules that are missing an electron. Because electrons prefer to travel in pairs, free radicals aggressively steal electrons from healthy molecules. The electron-stealing chain reaction that results produces compounds that cause cellular damage.

Free radicals are a natural byproduct of cell metabolism, the process by which cells use oxygen to create energy. Exposure to everyday environmental factors such as cigarette smoke, air pollution and sunlight also stimulate free radical production.

Scientists estimate that each cell in the body may get pounded with as many as 10,000 free radical hits a day! Your body does its best to counter free radicals naturally, but over time free radical build up takes its toll. It's no wonder that many scientists link free radical damage to cancer, heart disease, cataracts and premature aging.

Antioxidants counter free radical damage by supplying extra electrons that bind with and stabilize free radical molecules. Antioxidant-rich foods and supplements provide the body with the ammunition it needs to fend off the non-stop free radical bombardment. Some of the most commonly known antioxidant nutrients are vitamins A, C and E.

Phytonutrients

Phytonutrients or phytochemicals are nutrients from plants that promote a variety of beneficial functions. Many exhibit powerful antioxidant properties. Scientists are working feverishly to mine the largely unexplored potential that phytonutrients hold for medicine. Some of the research has revealed amazing possibilities.

One class of phytonutrient found in grape seeds, for example, exhibits antioxidant properties for up to three days in the body. More importantly, it is able to cross the blood-brain barrier. Brain tissue is particularly susceptible to free radical-induced oxidation. This phytonutrient also inhibits enzymes that break down vitamins C and E into less useful nutrients.

Some of the best phytonutrients are proanthocyanidins (grape seed extract), sulforaphane (broccoli extract), and lycopene (tomato extract).

Chelated Minerals and Trace Elements

Dietary minerals and trace elements support necessary biochemical processes that help your body burn fat, build muscle, strengthen bones, promote healing and deliver oxygen to the cells.

Proper absorption or bioavailability is essential for effective mineral and trace element supplementation. Minerals and trace elements are more rapidly absorbed by the intestinal tract when they are chelated - or wrapped - in an amino acid coating. Chelated calcium, for example, is absorbed 60 times more effectively than the calcium in milk.

Enzymes

All biochemical reactions are started or accelerated by a special class of protein molecules called enzymes. One of the best known enzyme supplements is lactase, which helps people who are lactose intolerant or unable to properly digest dairy products.

Bromelain is another enzyme getting a lot of attention for its digestive benefits. It's found in particularly high concentrations in pineapple. Bromelain is also being studied for its therapeutic value in treating severe bruises, inflammation and soft tissue injuries.

Pancreatic enzymes such as amylase, protease and lipase are also used to treat malabsorption syndromes, when the body's ability to digest a variety of nutrients is greatly impaired.

Herbs

In general, side effects from herbal products are minimal. Many consumers are entranced by the designation "all natural" and thus tend to believe that all herbal products are safe. They don't think of herbs as drugs.

The consumer should be advised by providers of medicinal herbs to observe the proper dosage recommendations and stop taking the herbal product if any adverse reactions occur. There isn't much information on herb-drug interactions, so people taking prescription medications should be cautious. The Botanical Safety Handbook published by the American Herbal Products Association contains labeling recommendations for 700 herbs commonly used in the US.

Herbal products have become more popular as consumers seek relief of common symptoms from sources other than their own physician. Therefore the majority of the burden of the safety of patients will fall on the practitioners of allopathic medicine (MDs) and the pharmaceutical industry.

Practitioners of allopathic medicine are now recognizing the widespread use of herbal products among their patients, and more clinical studies are likely underway. Allopathic clinicians, as a rule, aren't very familiar with the herbal agents, but will benefit their patients by being able to discuss these products with them.

It will be the pharmaceutical (drug) companies job to properly educate the physicians about what kind of popular herbs may cause adverse reactions when taken together with certain medications. The physicians will also have to have better screening forms and processes to find out what kind of herbs their patients are taking before prescribing certain medications.

Got Water?

Why You Need to Drink More

Are you drinking enough water? If you're like most of my patients, the answer is not as much as you know you should.

Water helps your body digest food, absorb nutrients, and transport those nutrients throughout your body. It's also a vital part of your body's waste removal system. Without adequate amounts of water, your body becomes dehydrated and cannot function properly.

More acute cases of dehydration can cause fatigue, nausea and dementia. Severe cases often lead to heat exhaustion, heat stroke and even death.

You don't have to run for hours in the summer sun to become dehydrated. In fact, most of us live in a habitual state of mild dehydration. Sure, we drink water every day, but it's not enough. Or, we think that drinking water-based fluids, such as coffee, tea or soda, is the same as drinking water. It's not. Coffee, tea and many sodas contain caffeine, a diuretic that dehydrates your body.

Make no mistake. Dehydration, however mild, can lead to serious health problems. If you aren't drinking enough water, over time your kidneys will pay the price. Your kidneys are an integral part of your body's purification system. Their main job is to clean your blood of toxins and metabolic wastes. And to function properly, they rely on a steady and sufficient flow of water.

The less water you drink, the more stress your kidneys suffer, and the less efficient they become. Over time, this chronic abuse can contribute to escalating health problems, ranging from increased likeliness of illness to painful kidney stones to kidney failure.

The bottom line: If you've been blessed with two good kidneys, take care of them by drinking plenty of water.

Flush Away Excess Body Fat

Drinking lots of water doesn't wash away body fat, but it does help your kidneys flush out the metabolic waste that is generated by burning excess body fat. Some of this waste is partially burned fat which passes from your body in stool or urine. So the more water you drink, the more urine you generate, and the more fat your body gets rid of.

How Much Water Do You Need?

The general medical consensus is about two quarts or six to eight glasses a day. You need even more if you exercise regularly or live in a hot climate.

The Best Way to Monitor Your Water Intake

Don't watch the amount of liquid going into your body. Watch the liquid that's going out. Take note of the frequency and color of your urine. As a general rule, you're drinking enough if you urinate regularly and the color is clear or a pale yellow. If you urinate infrequently or the color is a bright or dark yellow, your body needs more water.

Water and *Total Health*

Here's another reason to drink enough water...

Along with storing fat, excess insulin levels also promote water retention. As your *Total Health* program stabilizes your insulin levels, you'll start to shed this excess water. To stay hydrated, you need to replenish your body's water supply. Drinking the right amount of water every day may take some practice. Here are some tips to get you in the hydration habit...

- **Start your day with an eight-ounce glass of water.** Your body is always dehydrated after six to eight hours without water. The sooner you hydrate, the better and more alert you'll feel - before that first cup of coffee!

- **Drink an eight-ounce glass before breakfast, lunch and dinner.** Water before meals tends to take an edge off hunger.

- Reduce your consumption of coffee and other caffeinated beverages to one or two cups a day. Aside from its diuretic quality, coffee can also stimulate excess insulin production. Replace those extra cups of coffee with hot water. Add lemon for flavor, if you like. Herbal teas are also okay. Many people have discovered that sipping hot water or herbal tea is a remarkably effective way to wean themselves off caffeine. Reduce your caffeine consumption gradually to minimize the headaches and mood swings that often accompany caffeine withdrawal.

- **Ask yourself if you're thirsty.** Chances are you're much more thirsty than you realize. Asking the question forces you to become aware of your thirst. But you can't do anything about it unless you have water on hand. When water is out of sight, it's out of mind. That's why you should...

- **Take water with you.** Next time you're in the grocery story, buy a flat of 16-ounce disposable water bottles. Take one with you wherever you go...in the car, at work, on errands, when you go for a walk. When the bottle is empty, refill it. One way to keep track of your water intake is to place four rubber bands around the bottle. Each time you finish 16 ounces, take off a rubber band.

- **Get bubbly.** These days, supermarkets have entire aisles dedicated to bottled water products. For variety, put some plain or flavored carbonated water in your cart. Look for orange, lemon or lime flavored sparkling water. Stay away from carbonated water flavored with juice. You want the bubbles, not the extra sugar.

- **Monitor your water output.** The best indication that you're drinking more water is that you're urinating more frequently.

Don't think of this as an inconvenience. Think of it as a sign that you're doing your part to help your body's natural purification system keep you healthy.

Fiber Facts

Let's do a little word association. If I say "fiber" - what's the first thought that pops into your head? If you said "constipation," you're being honest. Most of us think of fiber as the stuff that keeps our bowels "regular" - what mom and dad used to refer to less delicately as "roughage."

What Is Fiber?

Fiber is the part of plant food that your body can't digest. Actually, there are five different kinds of fiber. Nutritionists divide them into two main categories: soluble and insoluble fiber.

- **The soluble fibers are pectin and gum.** They're found in foods such as beans, oats and citrus fruits. Soluble fibers dissolve and thicken in water.
- **The insoluble fibers are cellulose, hemicellulose and lignin.** They are found in foods such as wheat bran, nuts, seeds and fruits. Insoluble fibers include the outer coating of grains and the skins of fruits and vegetables. Insoluble fibers don't dissolve in water.

Why Fiber Is Good for You

Thanks to increasing scientific study, fiber is getting a lot more respect than it's well-deserved reputation as a natural remedy for constipation. The medical community now recognizes fiber as an essential dietary component with long-term health benefits.

- **Fiber helps prevent hemorrhoids.** Hemorrhoids are the painful swelling of veins near the anus most often caused by strained bowel movements. Fiber softens and adds bulk to bowel movements, making them easier to pass.
- **Fiber reduces the risk of heart disease by lowering cholesterol levels.** Fiber binds to cholesterol and evacuates it in the stool before its absorption into the blood stream.

- **Fiber helps regulate insulin levels.** Fiber diminishes the body's insulin response by inhibiting the absorption of glucose into the blood stream.
- **Fiber may reduce the risk of certain cancers.** For years, researchers have said that high-fiber diets may reduce the risk of colon, rectal and breast cancer. A number of explanations have been offered. One popular theory holds that fiber speeds up the passage of harmful waste through the intestines, minimizing their absorption and contact with intestinal cells.

How Much Fiber Do You Need?

The general medical consensus is between 25 and 40 grams daily. Most Americans get less than half that amount. That's why your *Total Health* program makes it easy to get all the fiber you need. You just don't get it from carbohydrate-loaded food choices that stimulate excess insulin production and fat storage.

On the *Total Health* program you can get your fiber - even when you go against the grain...

- **Choose your carbohydrates in the form of fiber-rich fruits and vegetables.** For a list of fruits and vegetables that qualify as fiber-rich carbohydrates, see the **Macronutrient Food Unit List.**
- **If you must eat bread or pasta, limit the amount** and choose whole grains.
- **Take your nutritional supplements.** It complements your protein-rich, favorable-carbohydrate eating program.
- **Take a fiber supplement,** such as Metamucil or other over-the-counter fiber supplements. Visit **www.lowcarboptions.com** for a complete listing of recommended fiber supplements.

A final tip: Increase your fiber intake gradually! Too much fiber can cause gas or diarrhea. To avoid these natural side effects, drink plenty of water.

Digestive Disorders "Silo Syndrome"

Growing up in the farm country of Wisconsin has once again come in handy! It's brought us the term I call "*silo syndrome*."

One of the first things I eliminate with patients during the beginning stages of the *Total Health* weight loss program are "high-glycemic" carbohydrates, such as pasta (made with flour and water), starchy white rice and potatoes, and excessive grains. All the types of carbohydrates which convert into sugar very rapidly.

Many of my patients who suffered from indigestion and other more serious digestive disorders also ate excessive amounts of these types of carbohydrates. Many of these same patients were also taking prescription medications prescribed by their gastroenterologists to help alleviate the symptoms of indigestion.

Within weeks of eliminating the flour and grains, their symptoms of indigestion started to fade. So much so, that many of the patients were able to reduce and even eliminate their medications for digestive disorders.

Upon further clinical evaluation and exploration of my Wisconsin roots, the answer was clear! The same process that takes place inside the tall round cylinders (silos) standing next to the barns on the farms of Wisconsin, was also taking place in the stomachs of my patients. A process called *fermentation*.

When farmers fill the "silos" with feed corn to feed their livestock for the winter, it starts to ferment. This fermentation process gives off powerful nitrogenous gases. These nitrogenous gases are so strong that farmers will sometimes become overcome (pass out) from the gases and even die. This happens when the unsuspecting farmer gets inside the silo to dislodge feed corn which becomes stuck in the grain chute.

These same powerful nitrogenous gases build-up in our stomachs and digestive tracts from the fermentation of flour, starches and other grains, during the normal digestion process. It's these same powerful nitrogenous gases that eventually irritate the lining of our stomachs and digestive tracts causing indigestion and more serious digestive disorders.

Hence, the term I call "*silo syndrome*" was born!

Some Final Tips: Here are a few handy tips for managing your weight over the holidays . . .

Powerful Tips for Reducing Holiday Food Cravings

Around the holidays I'm always asked the familiar question, "What can I have for holiday meals and still maintain a protein-rich, favorable-carbohydrate balance?" My response to my patients is not to worry about it and go ahead and enjoy your day. The key is to get right back to a healthy balance of proteins and carbohydrates the very next day.

Keeping your blood sugars under control through limiting excessive carbohydrate consumption helps to reduce your food cravings. Therefore you're less likely to continue eating your way through the holidays from Thanksgiving through New Years. Here are some powerful tips for keeping those carbohydrate cravings under control for the holidays:

- Be sure to eat an adequate amount of the main protein entrée at your holiday meal. This is usually in the form of turkey, ham, duck, etc. If you are unsure about how much protein to eat, you can use what I call the "ballpark" technique. Keep your protein choice to a portion a little larger than the size of the palm of your hand - roughly 4-6 oz.

- Go ahead and eat a small amount of each side dish. This would include sweet potatoes, mash potatoes and gravy, stuffing, cranberry sauce, etc. Even though we consider these forms of carbohydrates unfavorable, I want you to enjoy your day. Just eat smaller amounts of each.

- Enjoy a small portion of dessert such as pumpkin pie, etc. immediately after the main meal. If you wait to have dessert later in the day, do not eat it by itself. You must have the dessert along with a protein such as cheese to counter-balance the blood sugar response of the dessert.

- Make sure to send all of the desserts and unfavorable carbohydrate leftovers home with your guests. This will keep you from being tempted through the course of the day and remainder of the holidays.

Part III

Exercise: How to Get Started and Why

Not getting enough exercise? You're not alone. The number of Americans whose idea of physical activity is reaching for the remote control has reached crisis proportions.

In 1996, a U.S. Surgeon General's report estimated that 60 percent of adult Americans were not physically active on a regular basis. And 25 percent of adults - that's one in four Americans - were not active at all! In 1999, a follow up survey conducted for a non-profit weight loss support group reported that nearly half (48%) of Americans claimed to exercise regularly.

That figure - while encouraging - still leaves more than half of American adults on the couch. Is it any wonder that the number of people who are disabled or killed by obesity-related diseases grows every year?

If you're serious about living in total health, you must make regular physical activity part of your life. In this chapter, we'll take a look at how your body *and mind* benefit from a combination of aerobic, resistance and passive exercise. You'll also learn insider tips on choosing a health club and working with a personal trainer.

Why Exercise Is Important

The benefits of regular physical activity are astounding. For starters, exercise increases your metabolism to help you burn fat. Exercise boosts your stamina, strength and flexibility. It strengthens bones and improves your posture. And it lowers your risk of heart disease, high blood pressure, stroke and diabetes.

Physical activity also increases your self-esteem and confidence. You'll look better and you'll feel better about the way you look. It reduces stress, improves your mood and helps you sleep better. New research also suggests that exercise may even stimulate brain cell growth and slow the aging process.

Your body needs to move. If you don't use it, losing it is just a matter of time. As you get older, even simple tasks like climbing stairs will leave your lungs winded and your heart racing. Your joints will stiffen and your bones will weaken. Injuries will occur more often - with more serious consequences. Your range of motion will also suffer. You'll have to watch the way you bend over to pick up the paper. Turning your neck to back your car out of the driveway will be a struggle.

If you doubt me, I suggest you spend a day in a retirement community. Talk to people who've learned about the importance of regular exercise the hard way. They'll tell you that no matter how busy you are, it's a lot easier - and a lot less painful - to work with a personal trainer now, rather than a chiropractor or physical therapist later.

How Regular Exercise Burns Fat Faster

After thousands of *Total Health* consultations, I noticed that some of my patients made consistently faster progress towards their goals. What were these "fast track" patients doing differently? The "secret" was remarkably simple...

> *Patients who lost weight faster - and kept it off - made exercise a regular part of their weekly routine!*

While it's true that many *Total Health* patients lose weight just by eating protein-rich, favorable-carbohydrate meals, following a regular exercise program turbocharges your body's ability to burn fat. Here's how...

First, exercise boosts your metabolism - the complex biochemical process by which food is converted into energy. The lower your metabolic rate, the harder it is for you to burn calories. The faster your metabolic rate, the easier it is to lose weight. More about how to speed up your metabolism in a moment.

Second -and more importantly - your body has a powerful hormonal response to exercise.

Aerobic exercise, such as jogging, bicycling and swimming, stimulates the release of glucagon - the fat burning hormone - and inhibits the release of insulin - the fat storage hormone.

Resistance exercise, such as weight training, stimulates the release of human growth hormone - which burns fat and helps rebuild muscle.

When you follow your *Total Health* eating program *and* commit to a regular exercise routine, your body becomes a fat-burning machine. Thanks to your body's hormonal response to a protein-rich, favorable-carbohydrate way of eating, your high glucagon levels are already mobilizing stored fat to be burned as energy. Burning body fat gives you more than twice the amount of energy than burning sugars. The result is more energy for your workout.

The complete opposite is true when you "carbo-load" before a workout. Carbohydrates stimulate the release of insulin and inhibit the release of glucagon. Your workout is fueled by sugar, not stored body fat.

There is another benefit of high glucagon levels prior to exercise. Glucagon helps widen blood vessels, allowing your muscles access to more oxygen and nutrients. The result is a better workout and a faster recovery.

There are two basic types of active exercise: aerobic and resistance. If you want to lose unwanted body fat and gain lean fat-burning muscle mass, you need to do both.

Aerobic Exercise

Aerobic exercise works your heart and lungs to improve your body's ability to use oxygen as an energy source. The goal is to increase your stamina by training your body to work more efficiently and use less energy to do the same amount of work. The sooner your heart rate and breathing return to resting levels after a workout, the better your conditioning.

Aerobic activities are continuous and rhythmic, such as walking, hiking, jogging, bicycling and swimming. To benefit from aerobic exercise, you need to exercise at 60 to 80 percent of your maximum heart rate for 20 to 30 minutes at least three times a week. To figure out your maximum heart rate, subtract your age from 220.

There are two ways to measure your heartbeats per minute. One way is to count your pulse beats for 15 seconds, then multiply that number by four. The other is to invest in a heart rate monitor. Models vary in sophistication, from about $75 to more than $200. Go to www.fatburningbasics.com for a complete listing of recommended heart rate monitors.

Resistance Exercise

Pumping iron may seem like a mindless activity, but your body gains tremendous benefits. Resistance exercise or weight training builds your muscular strength, endurance, definition and tone. In the process, it also develops stronger bones and improves your posture. Most importantly, lifting weights accelerates your metabolism.

How many times have you heard someone say that the reason they can't lose weight is because they have a slow metabolism? Or listen to someone explain that the reason they never gain weight is a naturally fast metabolism? The implication is that your metabolic rate - fast or slow - is a matter of genetic fate and out of your control.

That's just not true. Metabolism is a function of muscle mass. If you have the metabolism of a napping snail, it's because you have a low ratio of muscle tissue to fat tissue.

This is why resistance exercise using resistance bands or weights must be part of your workout routine. The more lean muscle mass you have, the higher your metabolism. The faster your metabolism, the easier it is for your body to burn - and avoid storing - fat. Even when you're resting!

Resistance exercise tears down muscle fiber, which stimulates the pituitary gland to release human growth hormone. Human growth hormone is broadly recognized by the scientific and medical community as one of the body's most powerful hormones. Longevity experts believe it may be the key to reversing the affects of aging. It's also known as a ferocious fat-burner.

Human growth hormone mobilizes stored body fat to strained muscles, where it is burned as energy to repair torn muscle fiber. It's during this healing process that muscles gain bulk, tone and definition.

Resistance exercise fuels your body's natural fat-burning cycle. Human growth hormone burns more fat and builds more muscle, which makes it even easier for your body to burn more fat. And every time you lift weights, this amazing process repeats itself!

And you thought pumping iron was just for guys named Moose!

Passive Exercise

Passive exercise is essential for proper muscle and joint health. It increases your flexibility or your ability to bend, stretch and twist easily. It improves your balance and coordination, and it reduces your risk of injury. Regular passive exercise may even slow the progression of osteoarthritis and other degenerative joint conditions.

There are two kinds of passive exercise: Do-it-yourself stretching exercises and the muscle and joint mobilization performed by a qualified healthcare professional, such as a doctor of chiropractic. As you age, muscle stretching and joint mobilization will help preserve and improve your mobility and range of motion.

Stretching before and after workouts will help you avoid pulled muscles, cramps and a variety of other injuries. It will also speed your recovery. Moist heat and a skilled massage or physical therapist can do wonders to loosen knots and tight muscles.

Your joints also need special attention. As you age, calcium salts seep into the joints, causing accelerated wear much the same way sand wears down gears in a machine. This contributes to a condition called osteoarthritis, which over time, often leads to restricted movement.

Maintaining mobility is one of the keys to longevity and aging gracefully. Many entertainment and sports celebrities have extended their careers and preserved their range of motion well into their seventies and eighties thanks to periodic massage and joint mobilization.

Think of all the preventive maintenance it takes to keep your car running. Oil changes every 3,000 miles. New tires every 50,000 miles. A new timing belt around 75,000. Not to mention all the spark plugs, filters and fluids that are replaced according to the service schedule.

You understand that if you don't take care of your car it's only a matter of time before it breaks down for good. Now if money is no obstacle and you just can't be bothered with maintenance, when your car stops running, you can just go out and buy another. There are plenty of cars in the world.

The human body is the most complicated machine in the world - and you only get one of them. If you want to get the most from yours, take care of it. Give yourself the fuel you need. Exercise. And put yourself on a regular joint maintenance schedule. In the long run, you'll find it's a lot easier - and less expensive - to stay healthy than to keep your car running, anyway.

Choosing a Health Club

Choosing to start an exercise program is easy. Making exercise part of a lifelong commitment to fitness is another matter. The key is to schedule a regular time for exercise and then stick to your schedule until exercise becomes a habit. For most people, the *minimum* amount of time it takes to develop a natural exercise habit is six weeks. That's one-hour of focused exercise, three times a week for six weeks.

Too many people start exercising filled with unrealistic goals and expectations. And when they don't see dramatic weight loss, rock hard abs or "buns of steel" after a couple weeks, they get discouraged. They procrastinate. They get distracted by other priorities. Before long, they're back on the couch.

If you're serious about living in *Total Health*, and you want to make exercise part of your lifestyle, consider joining a health club.

There are a number of advantages...

- **Focus and Motivation.** Once you're at the health club, you've overcome the number one obstacle to sticking with a regular exercise program: showing up. Now, you have no more excuses. You're not distracted by the phone, the laundry, the kids or a myriad of household chores. You're there to work out. And so is most everyone else. It's really hard to procrastinate when everyone around you is in motion.

- **Equipment Choices.** Good health clubs invest in a variety of top-quality aerobic and resistance training equipment. You'll find several ways to get an aerobic workout or work a muscle group. That means its easy to try new exercises and equipment when its time to freshen up your workout routine. And the more choices you have, the easier it is to stick with your exercise program.

- **Relaxation.** If you want to give your mind a rest, put your body to work.

  Many of my patients report that time spent at the gym is deeply relaxing. Their focus is on simple physical tasks, such as lifting weights and breathing properly. Workouts are an oasis in a day of obligations.

  Is joining a health club expensive? Only if you don't use your membership. To make sure you choose a club that's right for you, consider the following before signing a membership agreement:

- **Location.** Join a club that's convenient to home or work. It's too easy to avoid working out if your club is too far out of your way.

- **Hours.** Will you be able to work out at a time that's convenient for you? Can you take advantage of less crowded off-peak times?

- **Cleanliness.** Check out the bathrooms and showers. Remember, it's supposed to be a *health* club. That means the facilities are cleaned regularly. Better clubs clean their changing, shower and restroom facilities throughout the day.

- **Staff.** Do the people behind the reception counter greet you with a smile? Do they make eye contact? Or are they too busy comparing tans and muscle mass to notice you? You want to feel comfortable asking these people for help. After all, you'll be paying for it.
- **Atmosphere.** Does everyone in the club look like a professional bodybuilder? Are there men and women working out? What kind of music is playing and how loud? Does the staff make an effort to "walk the floor" to answer questions or offer training tips?

  Each club has a distinct "personality." In this way, joining a health club is a little like having a roommate. Either you get along great, you put up with each other or you move out.
- **Stretching Area.** Is there a separate area to stretch before your workout?
- **Weight Room.** Are there enough free weights and weight machines to go around? What about cardiovascular equipment such as stairclimbers, treadmills, stationary bikes, rowing and skiing and elliptical motion machines? Is the equipment clean and in good repair? You want to be able to spend your time working out, not waiting in line.
- **Aerobics.** Does the club offer aerobics classes? If so, ask for a class schedule. If you plan on being the Sultan of Step or the Queen of Kickboxing, make sure the only class isn't offered at 5 a.m. Also, ask about the aerobics instructor's certification. Look for credentials from the American Council on Exercise, the Aerobic Fitness Association of America or the Exercise Safety Council.

Extras:

- **Sports Leagues.** Many clubs organize basketball, volleyball and racquetball leagues.
- **Swimming Pools.** Check chlorination levels and cleaning schedules. Are swimming and water aerobics courses offered? How many lap lanes are available throughout the day and during lessons?

- **Childcare Services.** More and more clubs are offering onsite childcare for parents who need someone to watch their kids while they work out. Many clubs contract with experienced daycare companies to maintain and staff the club's childcare facilities. Even so, make sure you check the childcare facility and staff with the same scrutiny you'd apply to a full-time daycare center. At a minimum, the staff must be certified for infant and child CPR training. Ask about fire, emergency and security procedures. Are staff required to have background checks? How often are toys and equipment cleaned? Ask about the sickness policy. Get the answers you need to have the peace of mind that your children will be safe and happy while you're taking some time for your own health and happiness.
- **Orientation Tours.** Some clubs offer free orientation tours to show new members how to use the equipment. Make sure the advice comes from a certified personal trainer - not the receptionist.
- **Personal Training Programs.** Many clubs offer one-on-one sessions with a personal trainer as an additional service. Working with a personal trainer is a great way to stay motivated and focused during your workout. Most clubs offer a complimentary training session and fitness evaluation to entice you to sign up for a series of personal training sessions. Others also throw in nutritional supplements and high-energy bars. But those incentives won't matter if you don't choose the right personal trainer for you. And that leads us to...

How to Choose a Personal Trainer

Health clubs are overflowing with free advice from well-meaning members. The problem is that much of it is misguided or just plain wrong. It can also be dangerous. Push yourself too hard on a treadmill, lift too much weight or use bad form and you're bound to hurt yourself.

Learning how to exercise safely and efficiently is a good reason for working with a personal trainer. Hiring a personal trainer also makes sense if:

- You want to stay motivated and focused.
- You want a fitness routine customized to help you reach your health goals.

These days, a lot of people are calling themselves personal trainers. The hard part is choosing a personal trainer who's right for you. Here are some tips and criteria to keep in mind...

- **Credentials.** There was a time when all you needed to call yourself a personal trainer was a good body and a business card. Today, professional personal trainers are certified by nationally recognized fitness organizations.

    Look for credentials from the American College of Sports Medicine (ACSM), the American Council on Exercise (ACE), the Institute for Aerobics Research or the National Strength and Conditioning Association.

- **Educational Background.** Want to work with a trainer who is committed to their profession? One indication is a bachelor's degree in health or exercise sciences. You also want someone who keeps up-to-date on fitness training and health information. Ask prospective trainers if they subscribe to any professional journals or attend continuing education classes or seminars.

- **CPR/First Aid Training.** If something goes wrong during your workout, can your trainer do more for you than dial 911?

- **Personality.** You are hiring a personal trainer to give you the motivation and information you need to benefit from a fitness routine. Being positive and enthusiastic is part of a personal trainer's job description. What matters is just how that enthusiasm is expressed through a trainer's personality.

    There's a huge difference between non-stop bubbly and non-stop intensity. You'll be paying this person to spend a lot of time with you, so make sure you have a good rapport.

- **Communication Skills.** An effective personal trainer needs superb communication skills. You want a trainer who listens to your needs and who takes the time to explain information in a way that you can understand. A trainer with a Ph.D. in exercise science is useless if they can't communicate their knowledge in a way that makes sense to you. There is no such thing as a stupid question. If a trainer makes you feel otherwise, find another trainer.

- **Gender.** Training is an up close and personal activity. Working with a trainer of the same or opposite sex may make a difference to you.
- **Fees.** Expect to pay between $50 and $100 an hour for a personal trainer. Ask about reduced rates for multiple sessions. What is the trainer's cancellation policy? How and when are you billed?
- **Availability.** Can the trainer accommodate your schedule? If you're not a morning person, don't expect yourself to get up at 5:30 a.m. to sweat with Sven.

Note: Additional questions about exercise or where to find a personal trainer in your area? Visit www.fatburningbasics.com.

Principles Behind Circuit Training

The concept of group exercise is not new. Arthur Jones, the inventor of Nautilus fitness equipment, first introduced circuit-training or group exercise concepts back in the 1970's, which are now becoming popular once again.

Fitness centers have been using the group exercise format for many years under many names (dance aerobics, step classes, cycling programs, etc.). The priciple is very simple: It's more fun to workout with your friends or others in a group scenario. Fun and camaraderie are key elements to the success of any group situation.

One of the fastest growing fitness franchises in the world offers a 30-minute circuit training course. All of the equipment is hydraulic and there are no weights to add or remove. The object is to keep the heart rate going so half of the time you are doing aerobics on boards or steps and half the time you are using strength training equipment.

This means you can get a complete fat burning, muscle toning, cardiovascular workout in just 30 minutes. The workout is performed in an interval circuit format (work/recover/work/recover) with timed intervals (usually 30-45 seconds) at each station. Usually a total of 9 - 13 resistance stations are used. These pieces use hydraulic cylinders designed to provide the amount of resistance you require for the type of exercise you desire.

Hydraulic resistance is the only type of resistance that is "accommodating" in nature. That is, the resistance matches the effort of the user, even as the user fatigues during exercise. The principle is similar to aquatics; the faster one tries to move fluid, the greater the resistance. You're much less susceptible to injury on this type of equipment. When (and if) you give out, it stops immediately. That's why almost anyone can perform this type of exercise (athletes, executives, busy moms, dads, kids, the overweight and seniors).

I was so impressed with the effectiveness and safety of this type of exercise, that I now provide this type of equipment for my patients at the *Total Health Weight Loss, Wellness and Chiropractic Center* in Thousand Oaks, CA.

The following are pictures of the hydraulic equipment and format used in our center:

Circuit Training Equipment

Hydraulic Biceps/Triceps Machine

Suggestions on Starting Your Exercise Program

Option #1:

If you haven't been involved in a structured exercise program in the past and finances aren't a problem, I suggest joining a local circuit training gym or health club with a certified trainer to show you how to exercise.

Option #2:

If finances are a concern or time is a factor, I recommend my *30-Minute "Fat Burning" Circuit Training Workout*™.

The following section includes photographs and instructions on performing proper warm-up and stretching exercises along with my *30-Minute "Fat Burning" Circuit Training Workout*™. I developed this program during my high school All-American wrestling days in the 1970's, which were based on circuit training exercise. This unique exercise system can be performed at home or on the road using a bungee resistance exercise band.

The 30-Minute "Fat Burning" Circuit Training Workout™

Congratulations for embarking on your new exercise program! I recommend exercising 3 days per week on Mondays, Wednesdays, and Fridays. This gives your body a days rest between exercise sessions. On Tuesdays and Thursdays you can go for evening walks, etc. after dinner for a relaxed form of enjoyable non-aggressive exercise. Weekends should be reserved for non-structured fun recreational activities of your choice, depending on the season of weather, such as golf, water-skiing, hiking, bicycling, swimming, surfing, snow-skiing, etc. This gives you a well-rounded and reasonable perspective of incorporating a healthy blend of physical activity into our busy lifestyles.

The *30-Minute "Fat Burning" Circuit Training Workout*™ consists of working-out all the major muscle groups by performing 9 different exercises. These include the back, stomach, shoulders, arms, legs, and chest. You perform 3 sets of 12 repetitions of each exercise in addition to walking or running in place with the resistance of the bungee device for 30-45 seconds in between each set of 9 different exercises.

NOTE: The work-out will take approximately 30 minutes if you walk or run for 30 seconds in between each set of resistance exercises or 45 minutes if you walk or run for 45 seconds.

Step One:
WARMING-UP

A proper warm-up enhances your body's vasodilatation (opening-up of the blood vessels) so that more blood supply is delivered to your muscles. Since warm muscles are more elastic, they're less susceptible to injury. Warm muscles also produce a fluid-like stretch that allows for a greater range of motion while cold muscles don't absorb shock or impact as well. Therefore it's very important to properly warm-up your muscles even before stretching your muscles prior to starting any exercise program.

The most common way to warm-up your muscles prior to stretching is by walking or marching in place while swinging your arms for 3-5 minutes. The best way to know that your body is properly warmed-up for stretching is when you begin to perspire lightly. Once you have begun to perspire you are now ready to begin your stretching routine.

Step Two:
STRETCHING

NOTE: When you begin a stretching exercise, go to the point where you feel a mild tension, and relax as you hold the stretch. **Do not bounce!**

Perform the following stretches in the following order:

Psoas Stretch: Bend the knees and flatten the lower back. Next bring one knee to the chest by inter-clasping your hands on top or behind the knee and start pulling with your arms until you feel stretching in the buttocks. Gradually straighten the opposite leg. Hold the stretch for 10 seconds and then repeat with the opposite leg.

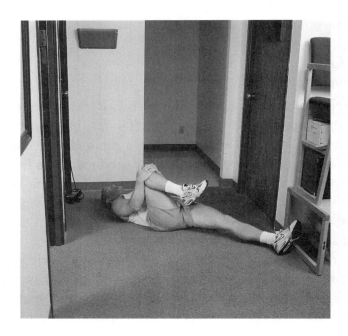

Low Back Stretch: Bend the knees and flatten the lower back. Next bring both knees to the chest by inter-clasping your hands on top or behind both knees and start pulling with both arms until you feel stretching in the buttocks. Hold the stretch for 10 seconds.

Twisting Low Back Stretch: Bend at the knees with both feet on the floor. Let your knees go to the left and your head and trunk to the right. Hold the stretch for 10 seconds feeling the stretch in the low back muscles. Repeat again for 10 seconds on the opposite side.

Back Extension: Lie as shown. Slowly push your upper body off the floor by straightening your arms. Breath deeply and relax your pelvis so that it drops down into the stretch. Hold the stretch for 10 seconds.

Hamstring Stretch: Sitting on the floor, straighten the right leg as you keep the left leg bent. The sole of the left foot should be facing the inside of the right upper leg. You are in a straight leg, bent knee position. Now, to stretch the back of the upper right leg (hamstrings) bend forward chest first from the hips until the slightest, easiest feeling of stretch is created. Hold the stretch for 10 seconds. Repeat again for 10 seconds on the opposite side.

Groin Stretch: Sit on the floor. Put the soles of your feet together with your hands around your feet and toes. Now gently pull your upper body forward until you feel an easy stretch in your groin area. You may also wedge your elbows in between your knees and apply a gradual outward pressure to achieve an additional stretch in the groin area. Hold the stretch for 10 seconds.

Foot and Ankle Stretch: Rotate your ankle clockwise and counter-clockwise through a complete range of motion with slight resistance provided by your hand. Rotary motion of the ankle helps to gently stretch out tight ligaments. Repeat 10-20 times in each direction. Next, use your fingers to gently pull the toes towards you to stretch the top of the foot. Hold the stretch for 10 seconds. Repeat again for 10 seconds with the opposite foot and ankle.

Arm and Shoulder Stretch: Sitting on the floor, bend at the knees and lean back on your hands with your arms stretched-out behind you. Next, lift-up your buttocks off the floor and rock slowly forward and backward feeling the stretch in your shoulders and the back of your arms. Rock back and forth 10-20 times.

Calf Stretch: Face a fence, wall, or something you can lean on for support. Stand a little distance from this support and rest your hands on the support above your head. Now bend one knee and bring it toward the support. The back leg should be straight with the foot flat and pointed straight ahead. Without changing the position of your feet, slowly move your hips forward as you keep the back leg straight and your foot flat. Create an easy feeling of stretch in your calf muscle (gastrocnemius). Hold the stretch for 10 seconds. Repeat again for 10 seconds with the opposite calf.

Step Three:
ATTACHING THE BUNGEE DEVICE

The bungee device consists of one 6 foot long bungee cord with a grip handle on each end. In the middle of the bungee cord is a nylon attachment loop strap which is used to attach the exercise device to a standard door knob or a sturdy railing.

DOOR KNOB ATTACHMENT:

When using a door knob for your attachment site, simply slip the attachment loop strap over the door knob and close the door securely with the bungee device pulling into the door frame.

RAILING ATTACHMENT:

When using a railing for your attachment site make sure the railing is sturdy. This will more than likely be the upright (vertical) post at the end of the railing which anchors into the floor. Hold both handles of the bungee device in one hand and hold the attachment loop strap in the other hand. Next wrap the bungee cord around the most sturdy portion of the railing. Then feed both handles of the bungee device through the open loop of the attachment loop strap and pull tight for a secure attachment to the railing as shown.

Step 4:
AEROBIC-WALKING OR RUNNING IN PLACE

Once the bungee device is securely fastened, to either the door knob or railing, we are ready to start our bungee exercise routine with walking or running in place. First, hold the handle of one end of the bungee cord in your right hand and the other handle in the left hand facing away from the door or railing attachment site. You may either have the bungee cord resting on the outside of your arms or inside of your arms, whichever is most comfortable to you. Next, walk away from the attachment site creating some tension on the bungee cord.

NOTE: The further away you walk from the bungee attachment site, the more tension you're creating on the bungee. Therefore, if you haven't been exercising regularly you should start out with less tension on the bungee in the beginning and work up to more tension later as you begin to get into better shape. This will help to reduce potential muscle pulls, soreness, etc. Also, be sure not to walk or run too much on your toes for this may lead to possible pulls or excessive soreness in the calf muscles of your legs.

Once you've created the desired tension on the bungee cord you may now start walking or running in place. After you've walked or ran in place for 30-45 seconds you're ready for your first set of resistance exercises (Step 5).

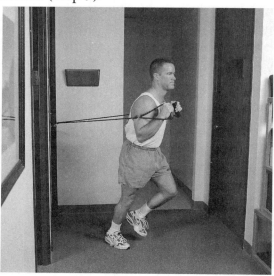

Step Five:
RESISTANCE-BUNGEE EXERCISES

There are nine different sets of resistance exercises designed to tone the muscles of the back, stomach, shoulders, arms, legs, and chest. 12 repetitions equals one set and you should perform three sets of each of the nine different exercises. In between each set walk or run in place. The nine different exercises and the order in which they should be performed are outlined as follows.

CAUTION: Not all exercise programs are suitable for everyone. Always consult your physician before beginning this or any other exercise program.

If anytime you feel you're exercising beyond your current fitness abilities or you feel discomfort, you should discontinue the exercise immediately.

ATTENTION: Any questions about what type of resistive exercise band devices you should purchase, where to find them, finding a local certified personal trainer or circuit training gym can be found at ___www.fatburningbasics.com___.

1. BACK EXTENSION

Leaving the bungee attached to the door knob or railing sit on the floor with your knees slightly bent facing the bungee attachment site. Next you should hold the bungee grip handles close together with your left and right hands overlapping each other. You should then pull the bungee handles to your chest. Remember the further away you are from the bungee attachment site, the more tension you will have on the bungee cord, so don't sit too far away from the attachment site in the beginning. Once you've pulled the bungee handles to your chest you should simply extend backwards against the resistance of the bungee cord as shown. You should feel the resistance in your lower back muscles when you're performing this exercise properly.

2. STOMACH CRUNCH

Leaving the bungee attached, sit on the floor with your knees slightly bent facing away from the bungee attachment site. Bring one bungee handle over your right shoulder and the other handle over your left shoulder. While continuing to hold the handles, inter-link the fingers of your right and left hands together while creating a tight grip of the bungee handles. Slide away from the bungee attachment site to create your desired tension and bend or crunch forward against the resistance of the bungee cord. You should feel the resistance in your stomach muscles when you're performing this exercise properly.

3. SHOULDER SHRUGS

Detach the bungee from the door knob or railing attachment site, hold one bungee handle in your right hand and the other in the left hand. Allow the bungee cord to hang down to the floor in front of you. Stand on the bungee with your feet approximately shoulder width apart. With your arms at your sides shrug your shoulders up and backwards against the resistance of the bungee cord. The closer your feet are to the handles on the bungee cord, the more resistance you will create. You should feel the resistance in your trapezius muscles when you're performing this exercise properly.

NOTE: Once you've completed 1 set (12 repetitions) of shoulder shrugs you will have to reattach the bungee to the door or railing attachment site to perform the aerobic portion (walking or running in place) of the bungee work-out. This also pertains to all other bungee resistance exercises where you're required to detach the bungee device.

4. ANTERIOR DELTOIDS

Leaving the bungee detached from the door knob or railing attachment site, hold one bungee handle in your right hand and the other in the left hand. Allow the bungee cord to hang down to the floor in front of you. Stand on the bungee with your feet approximately shoulder width apart. Now hold the bungee handles by squeezing them together in front of you with both your right and left hands . Pull the handles up to your chin against the resistance of the bungee cord. You should feel the resistance in the anterior (forward) shoulder muscles when you're performing this exercise properly.

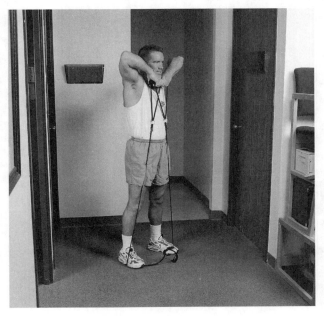

5. BICEPS

Leaving the bungee detached, hold one bungee handle in your right hand and the other in the left hand. Allow the bungee cord to hang down to the floor in front of you. Stand on the bungee with your feet approximately shoulder width apart. Now perform an arm curl against the resistance of the bungee cord with your right arm and then your left arm. You should feel the resistance in your biceps muscles when you're performing this exercise properly.

6. TRICEPS

Reattaching the bungee to the door knob or railing, hold one bungee handle in your right hand and the other in the left hand while facing the bungee attachment site. Next, continue to hold the bungee handles, bend your knees and lean slightly forward while backing up to create tension on the bungee cord. Now with your arms bent at a 45° angle next to your body, extend your right arm backwards and then your left arm. Your elbow joints act as a hinges while you straighten each arm against the resistance. You should feel this in your triceps muscles when you're performing this exercise properly.

7. SEATED ROWS

Leaving the bungee attached to the door knob or railing. You should sit on the floor with your knees bent facing the bungee attachment site. Next, while holding one bungee handle in your right hand and the other in the left hand, slide backwards creating tension on the bungee cord. Now simply pull the bungee handles to your stomach against the resistance of the bungee cord while maintaining an upright seated posture. This exercise is designed specifically to strengthen your lat muscles.

8. KNEE BENDS

Leaving the bungee detached from the door knob or railing attachment site, hold one bungee handle in your right hand and the other in the left hand. Allow the bungee cord to hang down to the floor in front of you. Stand on the bungee with your feet approximately shoulder width apart. With your arms down at your sides, bend your knees at a 45° angle and pull the bungee cords up waist high. Now, stand up straight. The closer you stand to the handles, the more resistance you will create. This exercise is designed specifically to strengthen your leg (quadriceps) muscles.

9. CHEST

Reattaching the bungee, hold one handle in your right hand and the other in your left and face away from the attachment site. You should have the bungee cord resting on the outside of your arms. Walk away from the bungee attachment site creating the desired amount of tension on the cord. Bend slightly at the knees and push your arms forward against the resistance of the bungee cord. This exercise is designed specifically to strengthen the chest muscles.

Part IV

Mental Health: Helpful Hints for Happiness

One of the principles of the *Total Health* program is that your mental health is just as important as your physical health. Here are some tips on how to preserve your emotional and social well-being and the importance of intellectual and spiritual growth.

Emotional and Social Well-Being

Seek and nurture healthy relationships. Choose your friends carefully. Look for people who value honesty and integrity. Look for people who build you up - not bring you down. Life is hard enough without inviting unhealthy, energy-draining personal and business relationships into your life.

Suppose you're a recovering alcoholic. In the past, you'd get drunk with the same group of friends on a regular basis. Now that you're trying to stay sober, you probably don't want to surround yourself with people who prefer to hang out in bars. And as much as you may like your old drinking buddies, the smarter choice is to cultivate friendships with people who understand your addiction and who support your decision not to drink.

When it comes to business relationships, it doesn't matter whether you're a doctor, a mechanic or a roofing contractor. Eventually, we all face situations that raise moral and ethical dilemmas. Your life is directed by the choices you make. It isn't always easy to make the right choice. The important thing is to realize that you do have choices!

Intellectual Development

Commit to a lifetime of learning - professionally and personally. Want financial success? Provide increasingly better service to your customers or clients. Keep up with your profession's or trade's new trends, techniques and equipment. Attend continuing education seminars. Read professional journals and books. It doesn't matter whether you treat patients or repair cars. Strive to become the best at what you do. Your investment will pay off in higher self-esteem, confidence, job satisfaction and income.

Balance professional development with personal growth. Stimulate your brain with hobbies and activities that spark creativity. Write, draw, paint, play music, play chess, dance, sing. Too busy? Give your creative time the same respect you give your professional time. Pull out your day planner and set aside time for fun!

Bonus: Spend quality time with the most important people in your life by involving your spouse, significant other or children in your creative endeavors. You never know when you might spark a shared interest. That's what happened to me when my uncle came to visit. He was an artist and he always brought sketch pads and pencils for me and my siblings. Then he'd teach us how to draw. When I was four years old, he taught me how to play chess. I don't draw like Rembrandt or play chess like Kasparov, but that's not the point. Thanks to my uncle's gift of time, I discovered two creative outlets that I enjoy to this day.

Spiritual Growth

Contemplate your life's purpose. What are you here for? When you aren't clear about your life's purpose, you're likely to pass through life without direction. This lack of focus often leads to poor personal and business decisions, poor career choices, relationship problems, depression, eating disorders, substance abuse and a host of other life-draining distractions.

When you're clear about your life's purpose, you can focus your energy towards achieving meaningful goals and dreams. Figuring out your purpose in life takes time and determination. Consider the following suggestions to help you get started...

Make time for self-renewal. Set aside time on a daily basis to reflect on your purpose, dreams and goals in life. If you believe in God or a higher power, you can pray for direction on how you can best use your talents to fulfill your purpose in life. It doesn't matter where you are - at home, commuting to work, on the golf course, in the shower - you can always take a few minutes to reflect on who you are, what you have accomplished in life and how you fit into the big picture.

Tip: Spend your self-renewal time focusing on love and goodness. Don't you spend enough time thinking about how much you have to do and how little time you have to do it? Isn't it demoralizing to watch the anger, injustice and violence on the nightly news? You cannot control the actions of others. But you can control your own thoughts and actions. Choose to dwell on what's right and good for a few minutes each day. It's good for the soul.

Love and serve others. This is one of the best ways to begin to discover your life's purpose. Regardless of your economic background, age, race or religion, you can love and serve others by showing concern and giving your time to people who are less fortunate.Most of us won't live up to the good deeds of Mother Theresa, but we can experience the same joy and goodness just by serving the people closest to us. Nowhere is this principle's power more evident than in it's ability to shape the lives of children.

How do we describe a parent's job? A parent *raises* or *brings* up a child. Think about that for a moment. The job description calls for parents to *raise* children, *to bring them up*. Not tear them down. One of the easiest ways "to bring a child up" is to praise them for the things they do right!

You don't have to be a parent to make a tremendous impact on a child's life. Do you know any single mothers or fathers who are struggling to raise children? Simple gestures, such as including their kid in your own family function, can make all the difference.

I know because it happened to me. My dad left my mom when I was seven. I had two older brothers and a younger sister. My mom had spent 15 years as a housewife. She had no marketable skills - and now she had to support us. She went to work for minimum wage. There was no money for child care.

Fortunately, our neighbors across the street were concerned about our sudden change in fortune. They went out of their way to keep a close eye on me and my siblings while mom was at work. And they included us in many of their family activities. I remember going water-skiing and snow-mobiling. My neighbors even took me on their summer vacations.

It meant - and still means - the world to me that they opened their family to me. Over the years, I've come to realize that in many ways, they saved my life. Without a father, and with a mom who worked all the time, I needed the security of knowing that someone cared. God knows what kind of choices I would have made in life if I didn't have that security and love to fall back on.

Maybe my late grandmother's simple advice sums it up best. She said, "Every time I get depressed or start to feel sorry for myself, I just do something nice for someone else. It makes me feel a lot better." Thank you, Grandma Markham!

Serve your community. Community service is another great way to love and serve others. If you have kids in school, get involved and help support programs that improve the quality of education. Help with after-school programs that offer kids positive activities that keep them out of trouble.

Community-based organizations such as the YMCA, Boy Scouts, Girl Scouts and teen centers help kids develop leadership and teamwork skills. They also promote healthy ideas about the value of service to others. Business and civic organizations such as Rotary International, Kiwanis, Optimists, Lions Clubs and American Legion also give back to the community by raising money for a wide range of community service organizations.

One More Thing. . .

All of us come from different backgrounds and different life experiences. These experiences can fill our lives with light and joy - and they can trap us in unhealthy and sometimes dangerous behaviors. If you suffer from behaviors or addictions that are keeping you from realizing your life's potential, you owe it to yourself and your loved ones to seek some professional help. If money is an issue, there are many city, county, state and federally funded programs that can help. There are also many 12-step support programs, such as Alcoholics Anonymous and Adult Children of Alcoholics, that meet on a regular basis.

Part V

Total Health Success Stories

The *Total Health* program works for everyday people, every day. If you're looking for inspiration and motivation, you'll find it in the following pages...

I Can't Believe I Waited So Long
Sandy A.
Teacher
Age 60

I'm one of those people who's tried all the weight loss programs. I'd go on Slim Fast for two weeks and eat nothing else and gain weight. I tried the Diet Center, but it was too restrictive. And for two years, I kept losing and gaining anywhere from 30 to 50 pounds on Jenny Craig.

The problem with a lot of these expensive weight loss programs is that you don't start with regular food. It's all packaged stuff. And all you think about is eating regular food again. I was scared to death of eating regular food, because I knew I'd be back to my old ways. And that's what happened.

Total Health is the first program I've been on when I'm not always thinking about how long until I can get off of it. That's because this really isn't a diet. It's just the way you eat. After a while, it becomes second nature.

When I'm invited to dinner, I don't have to worry about the restaurant or that there is nothing on the menu I can eat. You just choose some meat, some vegetables or a salad and forget about the rest. It's that simple!

The *Total Health* program has also done a lot to reduce my stress and increase my energy. I used to come home from teaching totally stressed and I'd forage for anything. I was hungry for anything. Stale crackers, it didn't matter. Whatever it was, I'd shove it in my mouth.

Now, I come home and have a cheese stick and water. Before I'd come home and zone out in front of the television. Now at the end of the day, I have something left for my family. I feel really good now. We take walks every night.

I began working with Dr. Markham in November 1997. I started losing weight over Thanksgiving and Christmas and kept going. More than two years later, I've kept off 26 pounds. My husband is following the *Total Health* program, too. He's also lost weight and his cardiologist has been astonished at the way his cholesterol dropped from 230 to 170.

The hardest part of the *Total Health* program was making that first appointment with Dr. Markham. Now I can't believe I waited so long to pick up the phone.

A Second Chance at Life
Brad H.
Age 49
Computer Specialist

I have two birthdays. The first was April 7, 1950. My second was August 16, 1985. That's the day I had my heart attack. I was 35 at the time. It was your classic heart attack. I was having dinner with my wife and a friend when the pain started in my left fingers and spread up my arm into my chest, which tightened like a vise. On the way to the hospital, I basically died in the back of the car. I was clinically dead until they revived me with those electronic paddles. People always ask how long I was gone. The only answer is 'long enough.'

When I regained consciousness, a cardiologist was standing over me with a clipboard. He started running down a checklist of lifestyle factors that cause heart attacks. The first question was 'How much alcohol do you drink?' I told him I didn't drink at all. Then, 'How much do you smoke?' I don't smoke. 'What about drugs?' I don't do drugs and never have. Period.

The doctor looked up from his clipboard. I was not making this easy. He wanted to understand why he was asking these questions of a 35 year old man who didn't drink, smoke or do drugs and who had no family history of heart problems. Finally he just said, 'Then, why the hell are you here?'

Good question. What did cause my heart attack?

In a word, "stress." In 1985, I was trying to move up the corporate ladder. Unfortunately, I was selling IBM typewriters in a world that was moving into computers. The fact that I weighed 240 pounds didn't help either. I knew I was about 30 pounds overweight, but I had always been a little on the heavy side. Besides, I was very active. Before my heart attack, I was actually running long distance, so I thought I was in really great shape.

There's nothing like death to give you a new perspective on life. You also get a lot of time to think while you watch your vital signs on the monitors next to your hospital bed. The way I saw it, I was getting a second chance at life. I had to lose the stress and the weight. It was a matter of survival.

Lowering my stress was the easy part. I quit my job while I was still in the hospital. The moment I did, the monitor showed my blood pressure dropping by 20 points. At first, I thought that losing the weight would be just as easy.

My doctors said to eat low fat foods and exercise. There was no formal instruction. As far as losing weight was concerned, I was on my own. For the next 15 years, I tried anything I thought would work.

I started with the Atkins diet, then the Diet Center and then Atkins again. Next I tried cutting all the fat, only to gain even more. At one point, I even went on a diet of grapefruit, eggs and spinach. I lost 85 pounds. But it all came back.

I was a human yo-yo. I'd starve myself on a diet. Then when I did eat, I'd eat twice as much. And the more weight I lost, the more I'd gain. There was never a moment I didn't think about food. Until I met Dr. Markham.

Ever since the heart attack, I've monitored my blood pressure regularly. One day at work it was up to 240/125. Given my history and my weight, which once again was at pre-heart attack levels, I was off to the Emergency Room to get checked out. I was told that if I didn't do something to lower my blood pressure, another heart attack or a stroke was just around the corner.

My company's nurse knew that I had worked out at the health club three to five times a week for years and never lost any weight. I was eating high quality food in reasonable amounts, but there was no weight loss. We agreed there was a clear connection between the food I was eating and my body's response to it. That's when she recommended that I check out one of Dr. Markham's presentations. Right away, I knew I found someone as passionate about my health as I was.

I started the *Total Health* program in May, 1999. Since then, I've lost 30 pounds without any sort of exercise whatsoever. My triglyceride count, which measures the amount of fat in blood, went from above 189 to below 50. And my blood pressure went from 240/125 down to 117/76.

I think of *Total Health* as an eating lifestyle because it's so easy to follow. The first day I had a headache from sugar withdrawal. But it went away within 24 hours. And from that day to this, I have never craved sugar of any kind. As long as you eat your protein and carbohydrates in the right combinations and portions, you can't go wrong.

Since I've adopted the *Total Health* eating lifestyle, I've dropped three notches on my belt. My metabolism has picked up and my mental focus has increased significantly. Best of all, I don't even think of food anymore. In fact, there are times when I have to look at my watch to remind myself to eat.

A New Way of Eating
Ellen M.
Physical Education Teacher
Age 50

In my profession, you are swamped with information about nutrition and exercise. It doesn't take long before you realize that no two experts really agree. So you have to go with what works for you, as long as it does no harm.

As a physical education teacher, I've always exercised daily, at least five and usually six days a week. Still, I'd always struggled to keep off an extra 10 to 20 pounds. Because I was getting plenty of exercise, I knew the key had to be what I was eating. So over the years I experimented with all sorts of diets. Most of them were different variations of the classic high carb diet, the stuff you'd always read in health and fitness magazines.

But following conventional wisdom didn't work. Losing weight on high carb diets was a struggle. In fact, I had to dramatically increase my level of exercise to keep from gaining!

I've seen a lot of fad diets come and go, so I was incredibly skeptical when friends invited me to one of Dr. Markham's free dinner lectures. I had already cut out bread and pasta for two weeks after glancing through The Zone. But that didn't do much for me, either.

I went to Dr. Markham's presentation out of pure curiosity. At the time I wanted to lose ten pounds. I wasn't planning on starting another program, but *Total Health* seemed so easy and straightforward that I had to give it a shot.

One of the things I liked about *Total Health* is the clear menu choices. I also like being able to eat things that are not on any other diet. I still can't believe that I can eat open-faced double cheeseburgers. The first week, I had one every other night and lost three pounds! After I dropped my ten pounds, I decided to go for ten more. And then another ten. I'd lost 30 pounds, but I was still cautious. In any diet, you can lose weight right away.

My trouble was that I always gained it back. That hasn't been the case with *Total Health*. I dropped 30 pounds and nearly two years later, I've kept it off.

The difference I've discovered with *Total Health* is that it isn't a diet. It's a new way of eating. From time to time I've indulged myself with higher carb foods, but I've always been able to get back on track just by following the program. It's as easy as eating my next meal.

At first, it's hard for people to understand that following the *Total Health* eating program really works. The medical and nutritional community are locked into the notion that the traditional food pyramid still works. But that's changing.

My physician didn't like what I was doing, at first. But when my cholesterol dropped from 187 to 120, even he was impressed. He asked me what I was eating. I told him I was eating a lot of cheese. He said, 'then you didn't eat much meat, did you?' I said, as a matter of fact, I did. He said, 'whatever you're doing, keep it up, because it's working.'

A Balanced and Sensible Approach to Weight Loss
Troy M.
Manufacturing Manager
Age 54

I had been on high blood pressure medicine for two years when my wife, my daughter and I began consulting with Dr. Markham.

Both my wife and I had read *The Zone*. But that book was too technical. Dr. Markham's *Total Health* program was easy to learn. We also liked that it takes a balanced and sensible approach to weight loss. You don't feel that you're cheating if you don't measure out everything you put in your mouth. And if you do drift from the program, you can get back on track quickly.

This is not a diet where you drop 10 pounds and then go back to your old routine again. It's a new way of eating. It's a lifestyle change. And the more closely you follow the program, the faster your new eating routine will become second nature.

Starting a moderate exercise program also gives you an edge. You can lose weight just by following the eating program, but if you exercise, you'll reap the full benefits of what *Total Health* can do for you.

Another key to our success was that we made a commitment to learn the program and set up a plan. The first thing we did is purge the kitchen of all the foods we didn't need to eat. If you don't have the stuff in the house, you aren't even tempted to stray.

Then we planned out what we were going to eat each week. We created our own custom menus from the food list using chicken, meat and fish and the favorable carbs that we liked. We ate the same foods, but in different amounts because each of us had different protein and carbohydrate requirements.

After I lost my first 30 pounds, my M.D. took me off my high blood pressure medication. I went on to lose a total of 60 pounds and I've kept it off now for 16 months. My energy level has improved significantly. I don't need as much sleep as I used to and I'm not groggy in the morning anymore.

My wife has lost about 50 pounds and my daughter has dropped 25. She's a freshman in high school and this program has helped boost her self-confidence. As her father, I'm happy she can start benefiting from good eating habits earlier in life. *Total Health* is a nutritional foundation that she can build on.

My Husband Says I Saved His Life
Jackie P.
Contract Manager
Age 53

It's hard to believe that you can go through so much of your life with the wrong information. I've tried losing weight most of my life and all these years I was eating the wrong stuff.

I didn't think it was possible to lose weight and feel good at the same time. Every diet left me feeling exhausted and lousy. Some of them helped me lose weight, but only while I bought their prepackaged diet meals. As soon as I went back to the real food world, it was a constant struggle not to regain the weight.

This program is different. For starters, I have a lot more energy and I feel great! *Total Health* teaches you how to change your eating habits. It's not a diet, it's a way of eating, and you learn as you lose by eating the right kind of foods in the proper amounts. Everything you eat on this program, you buy at the supermarket.

Total Health is very easy to follow. And I like having a coach who can answer questions and show me how to make the program work for me.

I've followed Dr. Markham's program for six months and lost 42 pounds. People at work have told me how much more healthy I look. My skin looks better. I've also updated my wardrobe to go with my new body.

My husband is on the *Total Health* program, too. He was seeing an M.D. every three weeks to treat his high cholesterol and blood pressure. His doctor prescribed medication and a low - almost no - fat diet loaded with pasta. He lost a little weight but his blood pressure and cholesterol didn't budge.

Then he started following the *Total Health* program. Within three weeks, he went to his regular checkup. His doctor was astounded that his blood pressure and cholesterol levels were all down to normal. To date, my husband has lost 60 pounds. He's off his blood pressure medication and only sees his M.D. every six months for monitoring.

My husband tells me that I literally saved his life. And he looks great! I've been married 30 years and it's like I have a new husband.

I Lost 21 Pounds in Four Weeks on Fast Food!
Bob P.
Insurance Broker
Age: 47

In September 1997, I discovered that serious blood pressure problems were going to delay some minor surgery that I needed. Reluctantly, I started taking blood pressure medication and for three months it brought my blood pressure under control.

Then it stopped working. My blood pressure spiked and I got so frustrated that I threw the pills out. I've always hated taking medications and to get me on blood pressure medication in the first place was like pulling teeth.

On a good day, my blood pressure was up to 157/105. Not horrible, but not good. I was about to go back to my doctor for a new prescription, when a good deed led me to Dr. Markham's *Total Health* program.

My mother had attended one of Dr. Markham's presentations and I'd agreed to take her for a free consultation. As a favor to my mother, Dr. Markham gave me a customized menu, too. No obligation.

I never expected this program to work. I'd been trying to lose the same 25 pounds for about five years. I've tried no-fat and low-fat diets. I've listened to all sorts of well-meaning, but ultimately bad advice about losing weight. And when I did lose weight, it always came back within a couple weeks.

So when I began dropping weight on Dr. Markham's *Total Health* program, I was floored! For one thing, the program seemed too easy. For another, I'd never lost more than two pounds in one week - no matter what I did.

All I did was follow my menu options and I lost seven pounds my first week! By week four, I'd lost 21 pounds. My waist sized dropped from 42 to 38.

Then one night I took my blood pressure. It was 125/82. I've been off blood pressure medication ever since.

The *Total Health* program is unlike anything I've tried before. I eat something every three hours, so I never feel hunger pangs. And I check in with Dr. Markham once a week to help me stay on track.

What I like most about the *Total Health* program is that it works in the real world. I work at a ferocious pace and I'm never home. The way my schedule is, I'm almost always using the fast food options. That's the part most people just can't believe: I lost 21 pounds in four weeks on fast food.

Since I started the *Total Health* program, I've completely revised my expectations of myself upwards. My weight dropped from 255 to 200 pounds. My blood pressure is down. My waist size is now 36. And I have the confidence and energy to start a regular exercise program. For a 47-year old guy who moves around as much as I do, I think that's pretty damn good.

Part VI

Total Health Recipes

Beef and Pork Recipes

Prime Rib

Type of Food: Beef

Ingredients
6 1/2 pounds prime rib roast (fat trimmed in one strip and reserved)
2 bulbs garlic, cloves peeled
1 tsp. salt
12 bay leaves
2 cups red wine
kitchen string

Instructions
Preheat oven to 450F. Puree garlic in a blender or food processor fitted with a steel blade. Add salt to garlic and process to a paste. Pat garlic paste in an even layer over top and sides of roast. Place bay leaves evenly over garlic. Place trimmed strip of fat over garlic and bay leaves. Tie in place with kitchen string. Sprinkle roast all over with salt and pepper to taste. Place in a roasting pan and pour red wine in bottom of pan. Roast 20 minutes per pound for medium done. Let stand 5 minutes before carving.

Serves 8

Nutritional Facts Per Serving
Protein: 28 Grams
Carbohydrates: 1 Gram

Oven-Baked Spare Ribs

Type of Food: Beef

Ingredients

2 pounds spareribs, cut into 3 pieces lengthwise
3 Tbsp. hoisin sauce
2 Tbsp. dark soy sauce
2 Tbsp. light soy sauce
2 Tbsp. honey
1 Tbsp. sherry
1 Tbsp. tomato catsup
1 Tbsp. Splenda(r)
1 clove garlic, chopped fine
aluminum foil

Instructions

Combine all ingredients but meat in shallow dish/pan. Add spareribs. Marinate overnight, turning several times. Line shallow pan with aluminum foil. Preheat oven to 350 degrees. Roast ribs 45 minutes. Turn heat to 325, roast for another 15 minutes. When shrinkage occurs, ribs are finished.

Serves 4 to 6

Nutritional Facts Per Serving

Protein: 24 Grams
Carbohydrates: 2 Grams

Mexican Steak

Type of Food: Beef

Ingredients
4 nice steaks (about 6 ounces each)
2 cloves of garlic, pressed
1 pound mushrooms, sliced
1 large onion, sliced
9 oz. beef broth
9 oz. red wine
green chili salsa, 4 small cans

Instructions
Layer baking dish with steaks, garlic, onion and mushrooms. Mix broth, wine and salsa. Pour over the top and bake at 350 for 1 hour or until done.

Serves 4

Nutritional Facts Per Serving
Protein: 42 Grams
Carbohydrates: 4 Grams

Company Flank Steak

Type of Food: Beef

Ingredients
2 pounds flank steak

Steak Marinade:
3 Tbsp. honey
2 Tbsp. vinegar
2-3 green onions (top and all)
1 tsp. garlic powder
1 tsp. fresh ginger root, grated
3/4 cup olive oil
1/4 cup soy sauce

Instructions
Blend all ingredients in the blender and marinate at least 24 hrs. BBQ steak with plenty of marinade. Delicious!

Serves 8

Nutritional Facts Per Serving
Protein: 24 Grams
Carbohydrates: 2 Grams

Beef with Bean Sprouts

Type of Food: Beef

Ingredients
1/2 pound flank steak, shredded
2 cups bean sprouts
4 Tbsp. olive oil
2 Tbsp. light soy sauce
1 Tbsp. sherry
1 1/2 tsp. cornstarch
1 tsp. salt
1 tsp. Splenda(r) dissolved in 2 tsp. water(if needed)

Instructions
Combine beef, 1/2 tsp. of salt, cornstarch, and 1 Tbsp. of oil. Mix well with hand. Heat 2 Tbsp. of oil to 400 degrees in wok. When hot, stir-fry beef 2 minutes. Remove, set aside, and wipe out wok. Heat 1 Tbsp. oil to 400 degrees in wok. Stir-fry bean sprouts. Add 1/2 tsp. salt. Stir-fry 1 minute. Add beef, sherry, soy sauce, and Splenda(r). Stir constantly for 2 minutes. If too watery, thicken with dissolved cornstarch.

Serves 4

Nutritional Facts Per Serving
Protein: 28 Grams
Carbohydrates: 2 Grams

Wok Beef and Broccoli

Type of Food: Beef

Ingredients

1 cup lean, sliced tender beef
2 cups broccoli stalks, thinly sliced across the grain
2 ozs. canned mushroom pieces
1 clove garlic
2 Tbsp. olive oil
1 Tbsp. cornstarch
1 Tbsp. soy sauce
1/2 tsp. salt
1/3 cup soup stock

Instructions

Toss beef in cornstarch and soy mixture. Stir fry garlic in oil; add beef. Stir fry beef and remove. Bring broccoli and mushrooms to boil with salt and stock. Cover wok, reduce heat and cook for about for about 4 minutes. Return beef to wok and cook briefly with cover removed. Serve at once.

Serves 2

Nutritional Facts Per Serving

Protein: 28 Grams
Carbohydrates: 10 Grams

Hungarian Goulash

Type of Food: Beef

Ingredients
2 pounds boneless beef chuck, cut in 1" cubes
3 large onions, thinly sliced
1 cup dry red wine
1Tbsp. olive oil
2-4 tsp. paprika
1 tsp. caraway seed
1 tsp. (or more) salt
1 tsp. vinegar
1/2 tsp. marjoram

Instructions
Saute' onions in oil until tender and golden; add caraway seed, marjoram, salt, and paprika moistened with vinegar; mix well. Add meat and brown nicely on all sides. Add wine, cover tightly, and simmer very slowly for about 2 hours, or until meat is tender. Add water during cooking, if necessary.

Serves 6

Nutritional Facts Per Serving
Protein: 28 Grams
Carbohydrates: 2 Grams

Beef and Mushroom Dinner Combo

Type of Food: Beef

Ingredients
1 1/2 pound stew beef, cubed
2 large onions, quartered
1 small green pepper, chopped
1 1/2 cups sliced mushrooms
1 large garlic, pressed or minced
1 can beef broth
1 cup water
2 Tbsp. shortening
2 Tbsp. flour
1 Tbsp. prepared mustard
1/4 cup ketchup
1/2 tsp. salt
pepper, generous dash
Tobasco sauce, dash

Instructions
Brown beef in shortening. Pour off fat. Add soup, water, ketchup, mustard, garlic, Tobasco and seasonings. Cover and simmer 11/2 hours. Add onions, cook 40 minutes more. Add green pepper and mushrooms, cook 20 minutes more. Gradually blend 1/4 cup water into flour until smooth. Slowly stir stew. Cook, stirring, until thickened.

Serves 4

Nutritional Facts Per Serving
Protein: 35 Grams
Carbohydrates: 4 Grams

Stuffed Pork Tenderloin

Type of Food: Pork

Ingredients
1 1/2 pounds pork tenderloin
4 ounces fresh mushrooms
1/2 tsp. salt
1/4 tsp. pepper
7 ounces roasted red peppers, jar or canned, drained
1/4 cup chopped fresh parsley
2 Tbsp. soy flour
2 Tbsp. olive oil
3 cloves garlic, minced
1 cup chicken broth
2 Tbsp. dry white wine or sherry

Instructions
Finely chop 2 oz. of mushrooms; slice remaining 2 oz., set aside. Cut the tenderloin almost in half lengthwise leaving a 1/2" hinge. Open in a layer on surface. Pound to 1/4" thickness, sprinkle with salt & pepper. Top with roasted peppers in single layer, sprinkle with parsley & chopped mushrooms. Roll up & secure with string. Combine remaining salt & pepper in bake mix; coat pork in mixture & reserve excess. Heat olive oil in skillet at medium high heat. Add pork & brown 2 min. per side; add garlic during the last min. Add the broth; sprinkle with remaining flour. Reduce heat to medium; cover & simmer for 20 min. Remove pork & keep warm. Increase heat to medium high; bring pan juices to a boil. Add sliced mushrooms & the wine or sherry; cook until slightly thickened. Serve over the porkloin.

Serves 6

Nutritional Facts Per Serving
Protein: 28 Grams
Carbohydrates: 5 Grams

Fresh Pork and Sauerkraut

Type of Food: Pork

Ingredients
3 pounds lean fresh pork, cubed
1 medium size can or jar of sauerkraut
4 to 6 garlic cloves, minced
1 cup water

Instructions
Cut lean fresh pork into bit size cubes. Drain sauerkraut and rinse with water. Melt pork fat trimmed from fresh pork in skillet and saute pork cubes in own juices until lightly browned . Add minced garlic, sauerkraut and water. Cover and bring to boil. Simmer for 2 hours or until meat is tender, stirring occasionally.

Serves 4

Nutritional Facts Per Serving
Protein: 42 Grams
Carbohydrates: 5 Grams

Peppers Stuffed with Pork

Type of Food: Pork

Ingredients
1 pound pork
8 small green peppers, minced
1 scallion, chopped fine
1 cup chicken stock
3 Tbsp. light soy sauce
1 Tbsp. sherry
1 slice ginger, chopped fine
1/4 cup water
1/4 cup oil
1 1/2 tsp. cornstarch, dissolved in 1 Tbsp. water
1/2 tsp. salt and 1/2 tsp. Splenda(r)

Instructions
Combine pork with salt, 1 Tbsp. of soy sauce, sherry, ginger, scallion, water, and cornstarch. Mix well. Remove stems from peppers. Cut holes at the top. Remove seeds. Wash thoroughly. Dry. Fill peppers with pork mixture. Heat oil in wok to 350 degrees. Stir-fry peppers 1 minute. Add 2 Tbsp. soy sauce, stock, and Splenda(r), Bring to boil. Turn heat down. Simmer 20 minutes. Thicken gravy with dissolved cornstarch. Stir constantly. Remove peppers to platter and pour sauce over them.

Serves 4

Nutritional Facts Per Serving
Protein: 28 Grams
Carbohydrates: 4 Grams

Poultry Recipes

Asian Lemon Chicken

Type of Food: Poultry

Ingredients
Four 3oz. skinless boneless chicken breasts
1/2 cup chicken broth
2 Tbsp. dry sherry
2 Tbsp. fresh lemon juice
1 Tbsp. soy sauce
1 Tbsp. chopped pared fresh ginger root
2 tsp. cornstarch
2 tsp. sesame oil

Instructions
In medium bowl, combine sherry and soy sauce; add chicken, tossing to coat thoroughly. Let stand 10 minutes. In small bowl, combine broth, lemon juice and cornstarch, stirring until cornstarch is dissolved; set aside. In large nonstick saucepan, heat oil; add ginger root. Cook, stirring constantly, 2 minutes. Add chicken; cook 2 minutes on each side, until golden brown. Stir broth mixture; bring liquid to a boil. Cook, stirring frequently, 1 minute, until liquid thickens slightly.

Serves 4

Nutritional Facts Per Serving
Protein: 21 Grams
Carbohydrates: 1 Gram

Barbecued Chicken

Type of Food: Poultry

Ingredients
One 2- pound chicken, skinned and cut into 4 equal parts
6 garlic cloves, peeled
1/2 cup white vinegar
1/2 tsp. freshly ground black pepper
Barbecue Sauce:
1/3 cup ketchup
1 Tbsp. light brown sugar
1 Tbsp. grated onion
2 tsp. cider vinegar
1 tsp. Worcestershire sauce
1 tsp. Dijon mustard

Instructions
To prepare marinade, combine 2 cups water, white vinegar, garlic and pepper in gallon-size plastic bag. Add chicken; seal bag, squeezing out air; turn to coat chicken. Refrigerate at least 2 hours or overnight , turning bag occasionally. Place grill rack 5 inches from coals. Prepare grill according to manufacturer's directions. To prepare barbecue sauce, in small saucepan, combine ketchup, sugar, onion, cider vinegar, Worcestershire sauce and mustard. Bring to a boil; reduce heat to low and simmer 5 minutes. Set aside. Drain and discard marinade; grill chicken 10 minutes. Brush both sides with barbecue sauce and grill 10-15 minutes longer, turning and brushing with remaining sauce, until cooked through.

Serves 4

Nutritional Facts Per Serving
Protein: 28 Grams
Carbohydrates: 4 Grams

Chicken with 40 Cloves of Garlic

Type of Food: Poultry

Ingredients
One 3 pound chicken, skinned and cut into 8 pieces
40 garlic cloves
1/2 cup chicken broth
2 Tbsp. olive oil
2 Tbsp. minced flat leaf parsley
1/2 tsp. salt
1/2 tsp. coarsley ground black pepper
1/4 tsp. dried thyme leaves
1/4 tsp. dried rosemary leaves

Instructions
Preheat oven to 350F. Spray a 9 x13 inch baking pan with nonstick cooking spray. In prepared pan, combine garlic, carrot and oil, tossing well to coat thoroughly. Bake 20-30 minutes, stirring every 10 minutes, until golden brown (be careful not to burn). Sprinkle chicken with salt, thyme and rosemary; place in baking pan with garlic mixture. Pour broth into pan; bake, tightly covered, 50-60 minutes, until chicken is cooked through and thigh juices run clear when pierced with a fork. Transfer chicken to serving platter. With slotted spoon, transfer garlic and carrot to food processor or blender; puree, slowly adding pan juices, until very smooth. Stir in parsley and pepper; pour over chicken.

Serves 8

Nutritional Facts Per Serving
Protein: 42 Grams
Carbohydrates: 2 Grams

Dijon-Grilled Chicken Cutlets

Type of Food: Poultry

Ingredients

Four 3 oz. skinless boneless chicken breasts
1 garlic clove, finely minced
3 Tbsp. Dijon-style mustard
2 tsp. fresh lime juice
1 tsp. teriyaki sauce
Ground pepper, pinch

Instructions

Spray an indoor ridged grill pan with nonstick cooking spray. In medium bowl, with wire whisk, combine Dijon mustard, lime juice, teriyaki sauce, garlic and ground red pepper. Dip chicken breasts into mixture,one at a time, coating both sides; place on prepared pan. Grill chicken, brushing with and remaining mustard mixture, 4 minutes on each side, until cooked through and juices run clear when pierced with a fork.

Serves 4

Nutritional Facts Per Serving

Protein: 21 Grams
Carbohydrates: 2 Grams

Macadamia Nut Chicken

Type of Food: Poultry

Ingredients
4 chicken breasts - boneless/skinless
1 to 1 1/2 cups crushed macadamia nuts
2 eggs, beaten
2-3 Tbsp. olive oil

Instructions
Pound chicken breasts until thin. Dip in eggs; bread in macadamia nuts. Heat oil in non-stick skillet. Saute chicken until done. Approx. 8-10 minutes.

Serves 4

Nutritional Facts Per Serving
Protein: 21 Grams
Carbohydrates: 4 Grams

Chicken Saute with Watercress

Type of Food: Poultry

Ingredients
10 oz. skinless boneless chicken breasts, cut into 8 pieces
8 cups watercress, finely chopped stemmed
2 cups onions, thinly sliced
1/4 cup beef broth
4 garlic cloves, minced
1 Tbsp. + 1 tsp. peanut oil
2 tsp. Worcestershire sauce
1/4 tsp. salt
1/4 tsp. black pepper

Instructions
In large skillet, heat 2 teaspoons of the oil; add chicken. Cook over medium heat 2 minutes on each side, until golden brown. Remove chicken from skillet; set aside. In same skillet, heat remaining 2 teaspoons oil; add onions. Cook stirring frequently, 3-4 minutes, until lightly browned. Add garlic ; cook, stirring constantly, 2 minutes longer. Add watercress to onion mixture; cook, tossing constantly, 30 seconds, until wilted. Transfer mixture to serving platter; keep warm. To same skillet , add broth, Worcestershire sauce, salt, pepper and reserved chicken; cook, basting chicken with pan juices, until chicken is cooked through. Arrange chicken on top of watercress; top with pan juices.

Serves 4

Nutritional Facts Per Serving
Protein: 18 Grams
Carbohydrates: 2 Grams

Mandarin-Stuffed Cornish Hens

Type of Food: Poultry

Ingredients
Two 1 pound Cornish game hens, skinned
1 large mandarin orange, peeled and sectioned
1/2 cup thinly sliced onion
1/3 cup balsamic vinegar
1 tsp. dried oregano leaves
1/2 tsp. salt
1/2 tsp. black pepper

Instructions

Preheat oven to 450 F. Spray a 9 x13 inch pan with nonstick cooking spray. In a small bowl, combine orange sections, onion, vinegar, oregano, salt, and pepper; stuff hens with an equal amount of mixture, leaving most of the liquid in bowl. Place stuffed hens in prepared baking pan; surround with any remaining stuffing mixture. Baste hens with some of the remaining stuffing liquid; cover pan with foil. Bake, covered, 30-35 minutes, basting several times with remaining stuffing liquid, until hens are cooked through and thigh juices run clear when pierced with a fork. Remove hens and any solid stuffing mixture to serving platter; set aside and keep warm. Drain pan juices and any remaining basting liquid into small saucepan; bring to a boil. Remove from heat; pour over stuffed hens. To serve, cut hens in half.

Serves 4

Nutritional Facts Per Serving
Protein: 42 Grams
Carbohydrates: 5 Grams

Spicy Chicken and Snow Peas

Type of Food: Poultry

Ingredients

10 oz. skinless boneless chicken breasts, cubed
1 cup snow peas (Chinese pea pods), stem ends and strings removed
1 cup minced scallions
1 Tbsp. Worcestershire sauce
1 Tbsp. chopped pared fresh ginger root
1 Tbsp. sesame seeds
2 tsp. Asian sesame oil
2 tsp. soy sauce
2 tsp. peanut oil
1 tsp. hoisin sauce
1 tsp. Splenda(r)
1 tsp. cornstarch
1 tsp. rice wine vinegar
1/4 tsp. crushed red pepper flakes
1/8 tsp. Asian chili paste

Instructions

In medium bowl, combine Worcestershire sauce, 1 Tbsp. water, the sesame oil, soy sauce, Splenda(r), cornstarch, vinegar and crushed red pepper, stirring until cornstarch is dissolved. Add chicken, tossing well to coat thoroughly; let stand 10 minutes. In wok or large skillet, heat peanut oil; add scallions, ginger and chili paste. Stir-fry 1 minute. Add chicken mixture; stir-fry 4-5 minutes, until chicken is cooked through. Add snow peas, scallions, sesame seeds and hoisin sauce; stir-fry 2-3 minutes longer, until snow peas are tender.

Serves 4

Nutritional Facts Per Serving

Protein: 18 Grams
Carbohydrates: 5 Grams

Herbed Lemon Chicken

Type of Food: Poultry

Ingredients
10 oz. skinless boneless chicken breasts, cut into 1/4 inch slices
1 egg white, beaten
1/2 cup chicken broth
3 Tbsp. plain dry bread crumbs
2 Tbsp. dry white wine
2 Tbsp. fresh lemon juice
1 Tbsp. rinsed drained capers
1 Tbsp. minced fresh flat leaf parsley
2 tsp. unsalted butter
2 tsp. peanut oil
1/4 tsp. dried thyme leaves
1/4 tsp. dried oregano leaves
1/4 tsp. salt
1/4 tsp. black pepper
Lemon slices to garnish

Instructions
In medium bowl, combine chicken and egg white, tossing well to coat thoroughly; set aside. In gallon-size sealable plastic bag, combine bread crumbs, thyme, oregano, salt and pepper; seal bag and shake to blend. Add 1 chicken slice; seal bag and shake to coat. Place coated chicken slice on large plate; repeat, using remaining chicken slices. In large skillet, heat butter and oil; when foam subsides, add coated chicken slices. Cook 1 minute on each side, until golden brown and cooked through. Transfer chicken to serving platter; keep warm. To same skillet, add broth, wine, lemon juice and capers; cook over medium-high heat 2-3 minutes, until reduced to about 1/2 cup. Stir in parsley; pour mixture over chicken. Serve garnished with lemon slices.

Serves 4

Nutritional Facts Per Serving
Protein: 18 Grams
Carbohydrates: 1 Gram

Fish and Seafood Recipes

Spicy Grilled Shrimp

Type of Food: Fish

Ingredients
2 pounds medium-sized shrimp
1 clove garlic, minced or mashed
1 Tbsp. vinegar
1 Tbsp. finely chopped fresh mint or 1 tsp. dried mint
1 tsp. each salt, basil and chili powder
3/4 cup safflower oil
1/4 tsp. pepper

Instructions
Wash, shell. and de-vein the shrimp (or use about 1 1/2 pounds frozen deveined large shrimp- they need not be thawed). In a bowl or glass jar, blend the chile powder with the vinegar, pepper, garlic, salt, basil and mint. Stir in the oil and shake or mix until well blended. Pour over the shrimp, cover the dish, and marinate in the refrigerator for at least 4 hours, or overnight. Thread the shrimp on skewers and grill over charcoal for 6 to 10 minutes (depending on size) , turning once and basting liberally with the marinade. (Or arrange unskewered shrimp on a broiler rack and broil in the oven, turning once and basting well).

Makes 50 appetizers, or 6 servings as a main dish.

Nutritional Facts Per Serving
Protein: 37 Grams
Carbohydrates: 1 Gram

Simple Sole

Type of Food: Fish

Ingredients
1 pound fillets of sole
1/2 cup mayonnaise
1/2 cup sour cream
1/2 cup grated parmesan cheese
Dash paprika
Dash salt

Instructions
Arrange sole in a single layer in a greased baking dish. Sprinkle with salt. Over fillets spread a mixture of the mixed mayonnaise, sour cream and parmesan cheese. Sprinkle with paprika. Bake at 500 for 10 to 12 minutes until fish flakes with a fork. Remove from oven and let "rest" several minutes. Serve with lemon wedges, if desired.

Serves 4

Nutritional Facts Per Serving
Protein: 42 Grams
Carbohydrates: 2 Grams

Shrimp with Garlic and Wine Sauce

Type of Food: Fish

Ingredients
1 pound large shrimp
5 cloves of crushed garlic
5 Tbsp. olive oil
3 Tbsp. white wine
2 Tbsp. chopped parsley, salt, pepper and Parmesan cheese

Instructions
Peel and devein the shrimp. Rinse quickly under running water. Heat the oil and saute the garlic for about 2 minutes. Add the shrimp and parsley and cook gently on both sides for about 5 minutes. Season with salt and freshly ground pepper. Add the wine and stir well. Serve on hot plates. Sprinkle with Parmesan cheese.

Serves 4

Nutritional Facts Per Serving
Protein: 21 Grams
Carbohydrates: 2 Grams

Shrimp Catalina

Type of Food: Fish

Ingredients
1 pound fresh shrimp, boiled
2 large ripe tomatoes
1 stalk celery, chopped fine
1/2 tsp. salt
1/4 tsp. paprika
Mayonnaise

Instructions
Clean shrimp and chill. Peel tomatoes, chop fine, add celery and combine with shrimp. Season with paprika and salt and add mayonnaise to moisten. Mix well and serve cold on salad greens.

Serves 4

Nutritional Facts Per Serving
Protein: 24 Grams
Carbohydrates: 4 Grams

Salmon Supreme

Type of Food: Fish

Ingredients
2 pounds salmon steaks
1/4 cup butter
1 tsp. Worcestershire
1/2 tsp. salt
1/4 tsp. paprika
Juice of 1 lemon
Pepper and minced parsley

Instructions
In a shallow close-fitting baking pan, melt the butter and then add the lemon juice, Worcestershire, salt, paprika, and pepper. Coat the salmon in the butter and place the steaks side by side. Bake in a 400 oven for 15 minutes; turn fish over and spoon some of the butter on top . Bake about 15 minutes more, or until fish flakes with a fork and no longer is translucent in the center. Serve sprinkled with parsley, if you like.

Serves 6

Nutritional Facts Per Serving
Protein: 24 Grams
Carbohydrates: 1 Gram

Salmon Fillets with Zinfandel Butter

Type of Food: Fish

Ingredients
3/4 pound boneless, skinless salmon filet (cut in 6 equal pieces)
1/4 pound mushrooms, sliced thin
1/4 cup butter
2 Tbsp. finely diced shallots
2/3 cup Zinfandel wine
Chives, finely cut

Instructions
Melt 1 Tbsp. of the butter in a 12 inch saute pan over medium heat. Add sliced and washed mushrooms and saute until lightly browned, about 6 to 9 minutes. Remove from pan, set aside and keep warm. Add 1 more Tbsp. of the butter to same pan and melt. Add salmon to pan, season lightly with salt and pepper and saute until lightly browned, firm and translucent at the thickest part. (open or cut to test), about 7 to 10 minutes total. Remove from pan and keep warm. In the same saute pan, combine shallots and Zinfandel. Bring to a boil uncovered until mixture is reduced to about 1/4 cup - about 4 minutes. Reduce heat to low. Add remaining 2 Tbsp. soft butter, little by little until melted and sauce is smooth. Place salmon on dinner plates. Top with mushrooms, spoon sauce over and garnish with chives.

Serves 2

Nutritional Facts Per Serving
Protein: 28 Grams
Carbohydrates: 4 Grams

Fish with Cashew Nuts

Type of Food: Fish

Ingredients
6 fish fillets
1/2 cup chopped cashew nuts
2 Tbsp. lemon juice
2 tsp. grated lemon rind
Flour
Butter
Parsley salt and pepper

Instructions
Put the juice and rind of lemon in a shallow dish and allow the fish to stand in the mixture for at least 15 minutes. Roll the fish in seasoned flour and fry in oil or butter until fish is tender. Remove the fish, set aside and in the same pan fry and lightly brown the cashew nuts. Serve the nuts over the fish and squeeze a little more lemon juice over the fish and sprinkle with a little parsley.

Serves 6

Nutritional Facts Per Serving
Protein: 28 Grams
Carbohydrates: 2 Grams

Fish Vera Cruz Style

Type of Food: Fish

Ingredients

6 red snapper fillets
6 Tbsp. olive oil
1 can (17oz.) tomatoes, chopped
1 tsp. Splenda(r)
1 tsp. chili powder
1 clove garlic, crushed
1 onion, finely chopped
1 can (4oz.) pimientos, chopped
2 Tbsp. chopped capers
3 oz. pitted green olives, chopped
1/2 tsp. Allspice
Salt and pepper to taste

Instructions

In a heavy skillet, heat 3 Tbsp. of the oil. Combine the tomatoes with the Splenda(r), chili powder, allspice, garlic,salt, pepper, and onion, and simmer in oil for about 10 minutes, covered. Coat the baking dish with remaining oil. Put the fish in dish; add pimientos, capers, and olives to the tomato mixture and pour over the fish. Bake at 350 F. for 30 to 35 minutes, or until fish flakes easily when pierced with a fork.

Serves 6

Nutritional Facts Per Serving

Protein: 28 Grams
Carbohydrates: 4 Grams

Ceviche

Type of Food: Fish

Ingredients
5 pounds Pacific Red Snapper (cut into 1/2 inch cubes)
1 medium bell pepper (diced)
2 1/2 cups lemon juice
1 1/2 cups lime juice
1/2 bunch fresh cilantro (chopped)
1/2 bunch diced green onions or scallions
1 Tbsp. white pepper
1 Tbsp. salt
1 Tbsp. granulated garlic
1 oz. Tabasco
2 oz. safflower oil

Instructions

In a large bowl, combine lemon and lime juices. Then add white pepper, salt, garlic, Tabasco and safflower oil. Mix well. Add the cubed red snapper, onions, cilantro and bell pepper. Gently mix well. Refrigerate for 12 hours to blend flavors before serving. Serve on chilled bed of lettuce, with slices of lemon and a side dish of your favorite salsa.

Serves 6

Nutritional Facts Per Serving
Protein: 20 Grams
Carbohydrates: 4 Grams

Vegetable Recipes

Asparagus with Pine Nuts and Cheese

Type of Food: Vegetable

Ingredients
4 cups asparagus
1/2 cup Swiss cheese
1/4 cup pine nuts
Salt

Instructions
Add 1/4 cup pine nuts (toasted if you like) along with a pinch of salt and cook, stirring, for about 30 seconds more. Pour into serving bowl. and sprinkle with 1/2 cup shredded Swiss cheese; stir until blended.

Serves 4

Nutritional Facts Per Serving
Protein: 14 Grams
Carbohydrates: 9 Grams

Creole Green Beans

Type of Food: Vegetable

Ingredients
1 can (14 1/2 oz.) stewed tomatoes
1 can (14 1/2 oz.) green beans
1 onion, sliced
3 slices bacon, cooked crisp and diced
1 Tbsp. chili pepper
Salt and pepper to taste

Instructions
Mix ingredients together and simmer until well blended.

Serves 4

Nutritional Facts Per Serving
Protein: 1.5 Grams
Carbohydrates: 8 Grams

Mediterranean Style Zucchini

Type of Food: Vegetable

Ingredients
6 small zucchini (about 1 pound), stem and blossom ends removed
4 Tbsp. olive oil
1 large onion, minced
1 medium-sized clove garlic,whole
1 stalk celery, minced or thinly sliced
1/2 green bell pepper, diced
1/4 tsp. oregano leaves, crumbled

Instructions
In a wide frying pan, combine the oil, onion, and garlic; cook, stirring occasionally, over moderately low heat until onion is soft; do not brown. Add celery ,green pepper, and oregano, and cook until vegetables are just tender; stir occasionally. Remove from heat; cover when cool. Split zucchini lengthwise in halves. Drop into 2 quarts rapidly boiling salted water and cook, uncovered, for 3 minutes after boiling resumes; drain. When ready to serve, add 3 Tbsp. water to onion mixture and cook, stirring , over moderate heat until simmering. Add zucchini and mix gently until heated. Salt to taste and remove garlic, if you wish.

Serves 4

Nutritional Facts Per Serving
Protein: 0 Grams
Carbohydrates: 8 Grams

Hot Broccoli With Olive-Nut Sauce

Type of Food: Vegetable

Ingredients
3 pounds fresh broccoli, trimmed
1/4 pound butter
1/2 cup slivered almonds (2oz.)
3 Tbsp. lemon juice
1 garlic clove, crushed
1(2-1/4 oz.) can sliced ripe olives, drained
Water

Instructions
Melt butter in a small skillet. Add almonds, lemon juice, garlic, and olives. Let stand 1 hour to blend flavors. Reheat before serving. May be refrigerated overnight and reheated. Place broccoli in a small amount of boiling water. Cover and cook until tender. Drain. Place in a serving dish. Pour sauce over.

Serves 8

Nutritional Facts Per Serving
Protein: 1 Grams
Carbohydrates: 10 Grams

Savory Sauerkraut

Type of Food: Vegetable

Ingredients
1 can (1lb.) sauerkraut, drained
1 can(1lb.) tomatoes
1 medium-sized onion, chopped
3 Tbsp. bacon drippings
1/2 tsp. caraway seed
1/2 tsp. Splenda(r)

Instructions
Fry the chopped onion in the bacon drippings until soft. Add sauerkraut, tomatoes, caraway seed, and sugar; mix thoroughly. Turn into a 1 1/2 quart casserole and bake uncovered in a 350 oven for 30 to 40 minutes to blend flavors.

Serves 6

Nutritional Facts Per Serving
Protein: 0 Grams
Carbohydrates: 8 Grams

Savory Sweet Peppers

Type of Food: Vegetable

Ingredients
3 red peppers (about 1 pound)
3 green peppers (about 1 pound)
2 Tbsp. olive oil
1 Tbsp. wine vinegar
1/2 tsp. salt
1/2 tsp. dried oregano leaves
1/8 tsp. pepper

Instructions
Wash peppers; cut each in half lengthwise; remove ribs and seeds. Cut each half in fourths lengthwise. Heat oil in large skillet. Add peppers and cook over medium heat, stirring occasionally, about 15 minutes, or until peppers are just tender. Gently stir in vinegar, salt, oregano, and pepper.

Serves 6

Nutritional Facts Per Serving
Protein: 0 Grams
Carbohydrates: 6 Grams

Sicilian Broccoli

Type of Food: Vegetable

Ingredients
1 bunch broccoli
2 cloves garlic
4 Tbsp. butter
1/2 C. sliced black olives
1/2 C. chopped red bell pepper
Parmesan cheese for topping

Instructions
Divide broccoli into flowerets and steam until cooked, but still crisp. Place in warm serving dish. In small pan melt butter, saute garlic and add sliced olives. Pour butter mixture over broccoli and sprinkle with cheese.

Serves 4

Nutritional Facts Per Serving
Protein: 0 Grams
Carbohydrates: 5 Grams

Stuffed Eggplant

Type of Food: Vegetable

Ingredients
1 large or 2 small eggplant
1/4 C. butter
1 medium onion, chopped fine
1 green pepper, seeded and cubed
1/2 tsp. salt
1 tsp. basil
1 can (1 pound 4oz.) tomatoes, drained
2 oz. processd Swiss cheese, cubed
1/2 C. pine nuts

Instructions
Cut eggplant lengthwise. Cut around eggplant 1/4inch from edge. Carefully cut and scoop out center, leaving a 1/4 inch shell. Cube center portion and set aside. Parboil eggplant shell in boiling salted water for 5 minutes; drain. Melt butter in skillet; add onion , green pepper, and cubed eggplant. Saute until vegetables are tender. Add salt, basil, tomatoes, cheese and pine nuts; mix well. Spoon mixture into eggplant shell and place in greased baking dish. Cover and bake in a 350 oven for 30 minutes or until eggplant is tender. Cut to serve.

Serves 4

Nutritional Facts Per Serving
Protein: 5 Grams
Carbohydrates: 10 Grams

Salad and
Dressing Recipes

Chicken Caesar Salad

Type of Food: Salad

Ingredients
4 chicken breasts
2 large heads romaine
2 eggs, boiled 1 minute and cooled
6 to 8 anchovy fillets, chopped
1 clove garlic
3/4 cup olive oil
1/2 cup grated Parmesan cheese
1/2 tsp. salt
Freshly ground pepper
Juice of 1 large lemon

Instructions
Crush garlic in a small bowl, pour over the oil, and let stand several hours. Cut up chicken, stir fry and set aside. Tear romaine into a large salad bowl, sprinkle with salt , and grind over a generous amout of pepper. Pour 1/2 cup garlic oil and mix until every leaf is glossy. Break the eggs into salad; squeeze over the lemon juice, and mix thoroughly. Add chopped anchovies, chicken, and grated cheese. Mix again.

Serves 4

Nutritional Facts Per Serving
Protein: 28 Grams
Carbohydrates: 8 Grams

Cold Asparagus Salad

Type of Food: Salad

Ingredients

1 pound asparagus, cut diagonally
4 cups water
1 clove garlic, chopped fine
2 Tbsp. light soy sauce
2 Tbsp. sesame seed oil
1/4 tsp. Splenda(r)

Instructions

Bring 4 cups water to boil in wok. Drop in asgaragus. Boil 1 minute. Drain. Rinse with cold water. Mix next 4 ingredients in bowl. Pour over asparagus. May be kept in covered jar in refrigerator about a week.

Serves 4

Nutritional Facts Per Serving

Protein: 0 Grams
Carbohydrates: 5 Grams

Cauliflower Salad

Type of Food: Salad

Ingredients
2 C. raw cauliflower broken into florets
3 Tbsp. chopped onion
1/2 C. chopped, pitted ripe olives
1/3 C. finely chopped green pepper
1/4 C. chopped pimiento
Dressing:
41/2 Tbsp. safflower oil
1 1/2 Tbsp. lemon juice
1 1/2 Tbsp. wine vinegar
1 tsp. salt
1/4 tsp. Splenda(r)
Dash pepper

Instructions
In medium bowl, combine cauliflower, olives, green pepper, pimiento, and onion.
Make dressing. In small bowl, combine salad oil, lemon juice, vinegar, salt,
Splenda(r), and pepper; beat with rotary beater until well blended. Pour over
cauliflower mixture and refrigerate until well chilled, at least 1 hour. Keep covered.
To serve, spoon salad into bowl, or, you can arrange on lettuce on individual salad
plates.

Serves 4

Nutritional Facts Per Serving
Protein: 0 Grams
Carbohydrates: 5 Grams

California Cole Slaw

Type of Food: Salad

Ingredients
4 cups finely shredded cabbage
1 avocado
1/2 cup thinly sliced celery
1/2 cup chopped cucumber
2 Tbsp. chopped green pepper
2 Tbsp. sliced green onions
1 Tbsp. chopped parsley
1 Tbsp. lemon juice
1/4 cup each mayonnaise and sour cream
1/2 tsp. salt
1/2 tsp. Splenda(r)
Dash each pepper and paprika

Instructions
Combine the cabbage with the celery, cucumber, green pepper, onions, and parsley. You may do this ahead; cover and chill. For the dressing combine the lemon juice, mayonnaise, sour cream, salt, Splenda(r), pepper and paprika; mix until smooth. If you make the dressing ahead, cover and refrigerate until serving time. Just before serving, peel the avacado and dice it. Add diced avacado and dressing to the salad and mix in lightly.

Serves 6

Nutritional Facts Per Serving
Protein: 1 Gram
Carbohydrates: 6 Grams

Avocado & Red Onion Salad Bowl

Type of Food: Salad

Ingredients
2 heads Boston lettuce, washed and chilled
1 ripe avocado
1 large red onion
4 oz. olive oil and vinegar dressing

Instructions
Break lettuce into bite-sized pieces into salad bowl. Peel avocado, and cut in large sizes into salad bowl. Peel and thinly slice onion, and add to salad bowl. Toss together with oil and vinegar dressing just before serving.

Serves 6

Nutritional Facts Per Serving
Protein: 1.3 Grams
Carbohydrates: 6.6 Grams

Sea Food Salad

Type of Food: Salad

Ingredients

1 cup flaked cooked halibut
1 cup flaked cooked crab meat
1 cup chopped celery
1/2 cup mayonnaise
1/4 cup chopped sweet pickle
2 Tbsp. lemon juice

Instructions

Combine ingredients and chill thoroughly. Serve in lettuce cups.

Serves 2

Nutritional Facts Per Serving

Protein: 12 Grams
Carbohydrates: 5 Grams

Curried Chicken Salad

Type of Food: Salad

Ingredients
1 pound diced chicken, light and dark meat
1 Granny Smith apple, diced
1 tsp. chicken base (no MSG)
1 heaping tsp. curry powder
1/2 tsp. garlic powder
1/2 tsp. coarse ground black pepper
Mayonnaise to taste

Instructions
Mix all ingredients to taste. Stir in mayonnaise according to personal taste.

Serves 4

Nutritional Facts Per Serving
Protein: 21 Grams
Carbohydrates: 5 Grams

Marinated Zucchini Salad

Type of Food: Salad

Ingredients
8 medium zucchini
16 cherry tomatoes
1 1/2 cups beef broth
1 (4oz.) can sliced ripe olives
Boston or red leaf lettuce

Zesty Marinade:
1/2 cup olive oil
1/3 cup wine vinegar
3 tsp. Dijon-style mustard
3/4 tsp. salt
1/4 tsp. pepper
3 Tbsp. chopped green pepper
3 Tbsp. chopped green onion
3 Tbsp. chopped parsley
1 tsp. dry tarragon

Instructions
In a wide saucepan, bring broth to a boil. Add whole zucchini. Return to a boil.
Cover and cook 8 minutes or until zucchini are barely tender when pierced with a
fork. Do not overcook; they will soften as they marinate. Prepare Zesty Marinade.
Remove zucchini from heat and immediately plunge into ice water to stop cooking.
Drain, cool and cut lenthwise into eigths. Place in a 9" x 13" glass baking dish. Add
tomatoes. Pour marinade over. Cover with plastic wrap and refrigerate overnight.
To serve salad, line a large platter or individual salad plates with lettuce leaves. Place
zucchini on top. Cut tomatoes in half and arrange around zucchini. Garnish with
sliced olives. Drizzle additional marinade over. Makes 8 servings. Zesty Marinade:
In a blender or food processor fitted with the metal blade, combine oil, vinegar,
mustard, salt and pepper until blended. Place in a small bowl. Stir in green pepper,
green onion, parsley and tarragon.

Serves 4

Nutritional Facts Per Serving
Protein: 1 Gram
Carbohydrates: 5 Grams

Oriental Cole Slaw

Type of Food: Salad

Ingredients
1/2 large head cabbage, coarsely shredded
4 green onions, thinly sliced
1/4 cup slivered almonds
1/4 cup sesame seeds
1 teaspoon salt
1 teaspoon pepper

Instructions
Lightly roast almonds and sesame seeds in saucepan on stovetop. Combine all ingredients. Toss with a dressing made of 3/4 cup of oil and six tablespoons of rice vinegar.

Serves 4

Nutritional Facts Per Serving
Protein: 2 Grams
Carbohydrates: 7 Grams

Creamy Garlic Dressing

Type of Food: Salad

Ingredients
2 medium garlic cloves, chopped
1 egg
3/4 cup salad oil
1/4 cup wine vinegar
1/2 tsp. salt
1/4 tsp. pepper

Instructions
In blender, combine all ingredients. Blend until creamy and smooth. Chill several hours or overnight. Serve on greens of your choice.

Makes about 1 1/4 cups

Greek Dressing

Type of Food: Salad

Ingredients
1/2 cup olive oil
1/2 cup crumbled Feta cheese or (farmer or cottage cheese)
3 Tbsp. wine vinegar
1/2 tsp. oregano

Instructions

Combine all ingredients. Chill several hours or overnight. Serve on greens of your choice.

Makes 1 cup

Italian Vinaigrette

Type of Food: Salad

Ingredients
3/4 cup olive or safflower oil
1/4 cup wine vinegar
1 large clove garlic, crushed
1 tsp. salt
1/2 tsp. basil
1/2 tsp. oregano

Instructions
Combine all ingredients. Refrigerate several hours or overnight.

Makes about 1 cup

Soup Recipes

Cold Guacamole Soup

Type of Food: Soup

Ingredients
1/2 C. milk
2 avocados
1 chopped green pepper
1 small chopped onion
2 Tbsp. lemon juice
1 tsp. sea salt
3 C. plain yogurt

Instructions
Blend all the vegetables with milk in blender. When smooth, add yogurt. Garnish with mint or parsley.

Serves 4

Nutritional Facts Per Serving
Protein: 7 Grams
Carbohydrates: 12 Grams

Gazpacho

Type of Food: Soup

Ingredients
4 large ripe tomatoes, peeled and chopped
1 large cucumber, peeled and diced
1 medium-sized onion, finely minced
1 green pepper, seeded and finely minced
1 cup tomato juice, cold water, or regular-strength chicken broth
1 small clove garlic, mashed or minced
3 Tbsp. olive oil
1 Tbsp. wine vinegar
salt and pepper to taste

Instructions
Mix the tomatoes, cucumber, onion, green pepper, tomato juice, vinegar, oil, and garlic; add salt and pepper to taste. Chill soup until icy. Serve well chilled. You may choose to put all ingredients in a blender and save a few minutes.

Serves 6

Nutritional Facts Per Serving
Protein: 1 Grams
Carbohydrates: 8 Grams

Zucchini Soup

Type of Food: Soup

Ingredients
3 pounds zucchini (approx.) cut up with skins
3 1/4 C. water
4 strips bacon, cut fine (don't pre-cook)
1 boullion cube
1 onion chopped
1 small clove garlic
Salt and pepper to taste

Instructions
Cook above until tender, about an hour. Put into blender and serve.

Serves 4

Nutritional Facts Per Serving
Protein: 5.5 Grams
Carbohydrates: 6.5 Grams

Protein-Rich Snack Recipes

Zucchini-Cheese Squares

Type of Food: Snack

Ingredients
1 clove garlic, minced
6 eggs, beaten
1 small onion, chopped
3 C. shredded Cheddar
2 1/2 C. shredded zucchini
1/2 C. salad oil
1/2 tsp. salt, basil and oregano
1/4 tsp. pepper
1/2C. grated Parmesan
1/3 C. bread crumbs 1/4 C. toasted sesame seeds

Instructions
Saute onion and garlic in oil until almost limp. Add zucchini and cook until tender-crisp. Mix eggs with bread crumbs, spices, Cheddar cheese and zucchini mixture. Spread into a greased 9 x13 baking dish. Sprinkle with Parmesan and sesame seed. Bake at 325 for 30 minutes or until set when lightly touched in center. Cool at least 15 minutes. Cut into 1 inch squares and serve warm, room temperature or cold.

Makes 10 dozen squares (120 squares)

Nutritional Facts Per Serving
Protein: 2 Grams
Carbohydrates: 1 Gram

Turkey Roll-Ups

Type of Food: Snack

Ingredients
1 ounce of turkey
1 green olive
Pinch of pimientos

Instructions
A great way to use left over holiday turkey. Slice turkey into thin strips. Wrap around small green olives stuffed with pimiento and spear with toothpick. Ready for dipping into your favorite sauce

Nutritional Facts Per Serving
Protein: 7 Grams
Carbohydrates: 1 Gram

Smoked Salmon Rolls

Type of Food: Snack

Ingredients
2 slices smoked salmon or 1 can smoked salmon
4 oz. cream cheese
1 Tbsp. lemon juice
1 Tbsp. grated onion
Freshly ground black pepper
Chopped parsley

Instructions
Have cheese at room temperature and mix in lemon juice, grated onion and a little pepper. Blend until very soft. Spread on slices of salmon and roll up like a swiss roll and cut into 2 inch pieces. Chill several hours before serving. Dip both ends of the rolls in chopped parsley.

Serves 6

Nutritional Facts Per Serving
Protein: 6 Grams
Carbohydrates: 1 Gram

Salmon -Stuffed Avocados

Type of Food: Snack

Ingredients
1 package (8oz.) cream cheese, softened
2 cans (7 1/2 oz.) salmon, drained
3 avocados, black or green skinned
1Tbsp. lemon juice
2 tsp. Worcestershire sauce
1 1/2 tsp. salt
1/8 tsp. pepper

Instructions
In large bowl, with wooden spoon, beat the cream cheese with the salmon, Worcestershire, salt, and pepper until fluffy. Halve avocados lenghtwise; remove pits. Brush cut sides with lemon juice to prevent discoloration. Fill hollow of each half with cream cheese mixture. Refrigerate until well chilled, about 1 hour.

Serves 6

Nutritional Facts Per Serving
Protein: 11 Grams
Carbohydrates: 5 Grams

Jiffy Tomato Stack Ups

Type of Food: Snack

Ingredients
Use 3 large tomatoes
4 oz. process Swiss cheese, shredded
10oz. package chopped broccoli, cooked and drained
1/4 C. chopped onion

Instructions
Cut tomatoes into slices about 3/4 inch thick. Sprinkle each lightly with salt. Set aside 2 Tbsp. of the shredded cheese; combine remaining cheese, broccoli, and onion. Place tomato slices on baking sheet. Spoon broccoli mixture onto tomatoes. Sprinkle with reserved cheese. Broil 7 to 8 inches from heat for 10 to 12 minutes or till cheese bubbles and tomato slices are hot.

Serves 6

Nutritional Facts Per Serving
Protein: 6.5 Grams
Carbohydrates: 6.6 Gram

Herb Olives

Type of Food: Snack

Ingredients
2 cups unpitted ripe or green olives
2 small hot , dried red chilies
2 cloves garlic
2 Tbsp. finely chopped celery leaves
2 Tbsp. drained capers
12 rosemary leaves
1 bay leaf
1 cup olive oil

Instructions
Place olives in a jar, interspersed with all the ingredients except oil. Pour in enough oil to cover olives. Cover jar and shake well. Refrigerate 3 or 4 days before using; shake jar several times during this time. Remove garlic if olives are stored for any length of time.

Nutritional Facts Per Serving
Protein: 0 Grams
Carbohydrates: 1 Gram

Ham Roll-Ups

Type of Food: Snack

Ingredients
1 oz. thinly sliced ham
1 oz. squares Cheddar or Swiss cheese

Instructions
Slice thin strips of ham, and wrap around Cheddar and or Swiss cheese squares. Use favorite mustard for dipping.

Nutritional Facts Per Serving
Protein: 14 Grams
Carbohydrates: 0 Grams

Crab Stuffed Mushrooms

Type of Food: Snack

Ingredients
8 oz. package cream cheese, softened to room temperature
1 Tbsp. chopped green onion
1/2 C. crab meat, drained and flaked
1/2 tsp. Worcestershire sauce
1/2 pound fresh mushrooms, cleaned, with stems removed
1/4 C. grated Parmesan cheese

Instructions
In a mixing bowl, combine all ingredients except for mushrooms and parmesan cheese. Stuff mushrooms with crab mixture, mounding the tops slightly. Sprinkle with parmesan cheese. Bake at 350 until filling is golden (about 20 minutes).

Nutritional Facts Per Serving
Protein: 2 Grams
Carbohydrates: 1 Gram

Beef Roll-Ups

Type of Food: Snack

Ingredients
1oz. thinly sliced roast beef
Olives

Instructions
Wrap beef around a stuffed green olive and serve with a sour cream and horseradish sauce.

Nutritional Facts Per Serving
Protein: 7 Grams
Carbohydrates: 1 Gram

Avocado and Crabmeat

Type of Food: Snack

Ingredients
1 avocado
1 can, (6 oz.) crabmeat
3 scallions, finely chopped
1 Tbsp. mayonnaise
1 tsp. olive oil
1/2 tsp. Nutmeg, salt and pepper paprika

Instructions
Chop avocado and add the crabmeat, scallions, mayonnaise, oil and nutmeg. Mix and serve in a cocktail glass over ice and sprinkle with paprika.

Serves 2

Nutritional Facts Per Serving
Protein: 14 Grams
Carbohydrates: 5 Grams

Part VII

Appendices

Appendix I

Commit to Health and Happiness

Here's one contract you won't have to run by an attorney. On the next page is your own personal contract for health and happiness. Make a copy of this contract, sign it, and read it daily. Use it to reaffirm your desire and commitment to live in *Total Health* and renew your pledge to participate in life to the best of your abilities.

Remember, it's your absolute right to be healthy and happy! It's my deepest wish that this book and the *Total Health* program helps you take the first step towards lifelong health and happiness.

Total Health
Contract for Health and Happiness

I, _____, hereby declare

that I promise myself and my loved ones to nourish my body

with a proper diet, and to enjoy the lifeling benefits of physical

and mental health through exercise, intellectual development

and spiritual growth.

This commitment will help me maintain and enjoy the

quality of life that I most certainly deserve for participating

in life to the best of my abilities.

Signed:_____ Date:_____

Appendix II

Total Health Before and After Photos

Lost 56 Pounds in 6 Months

BEFORE

AFTER

Steve L.
Publishing Executive
Age 34

Lost 72 Pounds in 8 Months

BEFORE

AFTER

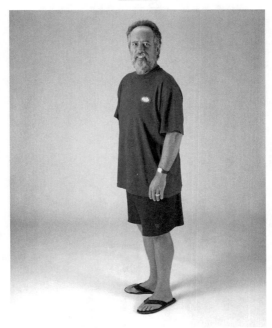

Greg B.
Insurance Agent
Age 49

Lost 50 Pounds in 4 Months

BEFORE

AFTER

Jerry K.
Retail Sales
Age 41

Lost 75 Pounds in 15 Months

BEFORE

AFTER

Barbara S.
Disabled, Rheumatoid Arthritis
Age 53

Lost 24 Pounds in 6 Months

BEFORE

AFTER

Judy A.
Account Executive
Age 60

Lost 52 Pounds in 7 Months

BEFORE

AFTER

Sue M.
Accounting Clerk
Age 59

Lost 57 Pounds in 5 Months

BEFORE

AFTER

George P.
Retired
Age 69

Appendix III

John Schneider Before and After Photos/ Larry King Appearance

Veteran television actor John Schneider tells his story for the first time about his struggle with childhood obesity on Larry King Live. The program he followed, resulting in his successfully taking off more than 50 pounds, closely resembled the *Total Health* program pioneered by Dr. Douglas Markham. Dr. Markham made his national television debut on this edition of Larry King Live, and told the nation about the importance of a protein-rich, favorable-carbohydrate way of eating.

John Schneider Before

John Schneider After

Larry King and Dr. Doug

John Schneider, Larry King, and Dr. Doug

Dr. Doug's and John Schneider's appearance
on CNN's "Larry King Live"

Appendix IV

HEALTH Across America Tour Photos

Some highlights from Dr. Doug's "*HEALTH Across America Tour*," part of a national public education campaign on the prevention of obesity-related diseases. This tour will eventually take him to America's 25 "fattest cities" as ranked by *Men's Fitness* magazine.

Dr. Doug with Troy Leinen, manager of human resources, Michael Willmering, V.P. of human resources, and Karen Lehman, R.N., occupational health services, *Bombardier Aerospace/Lear Jet*

Dr. Doug lecturing to the "wing assembly" unit about obesity and how to take control of their health. *Bombardier Aerospace/Lear Jet*

Dr. Doug posing with *Bombardier Aerospace/Lear Jet employees* as they proudly display their Carbolite® Sugar-Free Chocolate bars and DaVinci® Sugar-Free Syrups.

Carbolite Foods® and DaVinci Gourmet® have generously committed to donating their delicious low carb sample products to company employees along the *HEALTH Across America Tour.*

Dr. Doug taking a station break during a radio interview with *KNSS Radio* talk show host Steve McIntosh. Dr. Doug and Steve discussed adult and childhood obesity issues.

Dr. Doug with Sharon Poer, R.N., occupational health nurse/safety director, and Larry K. Wilkinson, M.D., occupational health physician, *York International*

Dr. Doug with Stephen Donowick, manager of human resources, *York International*

Dr. Doug posing with *York International* employees as they proudly display their Carbolite® Sugar-Free Chocolate bars and DaVinci® Sugar-Free Syrups.

Marleece Barber, M.D., medical director, *Lockheed Martin Space Systems/NASA* and Dr. Doug pose with the space shuttle in the background.

Marleece Barber, M.D., medical director, Holly Hebert, L.R.T., wellness support, Dr. Doug, Iris Davis, R.N., nursing supervisor, and Sharon Bollinger, adminsistrative assistant, *Lockheed Martin Space Systems/NASA*

Dr. Doug with Barb Essie, wellness director, *American Family Insurance Company* at their corporate headquarters. They discussed how to reduce obesity-related health care costs in the workplace.

Dr. Doug with Dr. Nabil Seyam, health, safety and environmental director, Toni Herbst, R.N., occupational health, *The Coleman Company*

Dr. Doug and Sherry Klinkner, community relations manager, *Barnes & Noble Booksellers*, after a successful lecture and book signing event. Sherry went on to lose 30 pounds in 4 months!

She went from 125 to 95 pounds on the *Total Health* plan with the help of the online support system at www.totalhealthdoc.com.

Dr. Doug poses with Madison Public Library supervisors Margie Navarre-Saaf and Ann Michalski after a community health lecture at the Alicia Ashman Memorial Library. Dr. Doug donated his book *Total Health* to all of the branches of the Madison City Public Library System.

Dr. Doug stands with library directors of the Brodhead Public School System Kris Brugger and Char Baumgartner. They are proudly displaying Dr. Doug's book *Total Health* after a lecture and book signing event at the *Barnes & Noble Booksellers* in Madison, WI.

Dr. Doug was a 1979 graduate of Brodhead High School in Brodhead, WI. He donated books to all of the Brodhead School System libraries.

Bibliography

Alpers D, Clouse RE, Stenson WF, eds. *Manual of Nutritional Therapeutics, 2nd ed.* Boston, MA: Little Brown, 1998.

Anderson, Bob. *Stretching.* Bolinas: Shelter Publications, 1984.

Audette, Ray with Troy Gilchrist. *Neanderthin: Eat Like a Caveman to Achieve a Lean, Strong, Healthy Body.* New York: St. Martins Press, 1999.

Brzycki, Matt. *Maximize Your Training: Insights from Leading Strength and Fitness Professionals.* Chicago: Masters Press, 2000.

D'Adamo, Peter with Catherine Whitney. *Eat Right for Your Type: The Individualized Diet Solution to Staying Healthy, Living Longer & Achieving Your Ideal Weight.* New York: G.P. Putnam, 1996.

Daoust, Joyce and Gene Daoust. *40-30-30 Fat Burning Nutrition: The Dietary Hormonal Connection to Permanent Weight Loss and Better Health.* Del Mar, California: Wharton Publishing, 1996.

Dufty, William. *Sugar Blues.* New York: Warner Books, 1976.

Eades, Michael and Mary Eades. *Protein Power.* New York: Bantam Books, 1996.

Erasmus, Udo. *Fats and Oils: The Complete Guide to Fats and Oils in Health and Nutrition.* Vancouver: Alive Books, 1986.

Gittleman, Ann. *The 40-30-30 Phenomenon: The Easy-to-Follow Diet Plan Tailored for Individual Needs.* New Canaan, Connecticut: Keats Publishing, 1997.

Guyton, Arthur. *Textbook of Medical Physiology, 7th ed.* Philadelphia: W.B. Saunders, 1986.

Haas, Robert. *Eat to Win: The Sports Nutrition Bible.* New York: Rawson Associates, 1983.

Hecker, Arthur ed. *Clinics in Sports Medicine: Nutritional Aspects of Exercise.* Philadelphia: W.B. Saunders Company, 1984.

Heller, Richard and Rachael Heller. *The Carbohydrate Addict's Diet: The Lifelong Solution to Yo-Yo Dieting.* New York: Penguin, 1991.

Heller, Richard and Rachael Heller. *Carbohydrate-Addicted Kids: Help Your Child or Teen Break Free of Junk Food and Sugar Cravings - for Life!* New York: HarperCollins, 1997.

Lemon, PW. Effects of exercise on dietary protein requirements. *Int J Sports Nutri* 1998;8:426-47.

Neporent, Liz and Suzanne Schlosberg. *Weight Training for Dummies.* New York: IDG Books Worldwide, 1997.

Poortmans R, Dellaliux O. Do regular high-protein diets have potential health risk on healthy kidney functions in athletes? *Int J Sports Nutri and Exerc & Metab* 2000;10(1):28-38.

Sears, Barry with Bill Lawren. *The Zone: A Dietary Road Map to Lose Weight Permanently, Reset Your Genetic Code, Prevent Disease, Achieve Maximum Physical Performance, Enhance Mental Productivity.* New York: ReganBooks, 1995.

Sizer, Frances, and Eleanor Whitney. *Nutrition: Concepts and Controversies,* 6th ed. St. Paul: West Publishing Company, 1994.

U.S. Food and Nutrition Board. *Recommended Dietary Allowances.* Washington, D.C.: National Academy Press, 1989.

Vigilante, Kevin and Mary Flynn. *Low-Fat Lies: High Fat Frauds & the Healthiest Diet in the World.* Washington: Lifeline Press, 1999.

Weil, Andrew. *Natural Health, Natural Medicine: A Comprehensive Manual for Wellness and Self-Care.* New York: Houghton Mifflin, 1995.

Weil, Andrew. *Eating Well for Optimum Health: The Essential Guide to Food, Diet, and Nutrition.* New York: Alfred A. Knopf, 2000.

Zarins, Bertram, ed. *Clinics in Sports Medicine: Olympic Sports Medicine.* Philadelphia: W.B. Saunders Company, 1983.

Index

Looking for Low Carbohydrate Products?

Visit **www.lowcarboptions.com** for recommended low carbohydrate products, sugar-free options, nutritional supplements for diet and health, and more . . .

Need Personalized Help or Questions About Your Weight Loss and Wellness Program?

Visit **www.totalhealthdoc.com** for your free one-month membership for personalized weight loss and wellness guidance via e-mail, over 120 recipes and more . . .

* Dieters who received personalized weight loss guidance via e-mail shed more pounds than those who didn't get extra help, according to an updated study by researchers at the Brown University School of Medicine in Providence.

Additional Questions About Exercise, Where to Find a Certified Personal Trainer or Circuit Training Gym in Your Area, Home Exercise Equipment?

Visit **www.fatburningbasics.com**.

Would You Like to Share Your Success Story, Want the Latest Updates or Additional Copies of Beyond Atkins?

Visit **www.beyondatkins.com**.

Beyond Atkins: A Healthier More Balanced Approach to a Low Carbohydrate Way of Eating is also available wherever books are sold or by phone at (800) 891-5165.

A portion of the proceeds from the sale of this book will be contributed to the Partnership for Total Health, a non-profit educational organization committed to promoting the health benefits of a protein-rich, favorable carbohydrate way of eating. To learn more about the work of the organization, visit www.partnershipfortotalhealth.org.